International Journal on Advances in Telecommunications

2016 vol. 9 nr. 3&4

Printed from e-media with permission by:

Curran Associates, Inc.
57 Morehouse Lane
Red Hook, NY 12571

Some format issues inherent in the e-media version may also appear in this print version.

Printed by Curran Associates, Inc. (2018)

International Academy, Research, and Industry Association (IARIA)
412 Derby Way
Wilmington, DE 19810

Phone: (408) 893-6407
Fax: (408) 527-6351

petre@iaria.org

Additional copies of this publication are available from:

Curran Associates, Inc.
57 Morehouse Lane
Red Hook, NY 12571 USA
Phone: 845-758-0400
Fax: 845-758-2633
Email: curran@proceedings.com
Web: www.proceedings.com

The *International Journal on Advances in Telecommunications* is published by IARIA.
ISSN: 1942-2601
journals site: http://www.iariajournals.org
contact: petre@iaria.org

Sponsored by IARIA
www.iaria.org

International Journal on Advances in Telecommunications
Volume 9, Number 3 & 4, 2016

Huaqun Guo, Institute for Infocomm Research, A*STAR, Singapore
Song Guo, University of Aizu, Japan
Kamal Harb, KFUPM, Saudi Arabia
Ching-Hsien (Robert) Hsu, Chung Hua University, Taiwan
Javier Ibanez-Guzman, Renault S.A., France
Lamiaa Fattouh Ibrahim, King Abdul Aziz University, Saudi Arabia
Theodoros Iliou, University of the Aegean, Greece
Mohsen Jahanshahi, Islamic Azad University, Iran
Antonio Jara, University of Murcia, Spain
Carlos Juiz, Universitat de les Illes Balears, Spain
Adrian Kacso, Universität Siegen, Germany
György Kálmán, Gjøvik University College, Norway
Eleni Kaplani, Technological Educational Institute of Patras, Greece
Behrouz Khoshnevis, University of Toronto, Canada
Ki Hong Kim, ETRI: Electronics and Telecommunications Research Institute, Korea
Atsushi Koike, Seikei University, Japan
Ousmane Kone, UPPA - University of Bordeaux, France
Dragana Krstic, University of Nis, Serbia
Archana Kumar, Delhi Institute of Technology & Management, Haryana, India
Romain Laborde, University Paul Sabatier (Toulouse III), France
Massimiliano Laddomada, Texas A&M University-Texarkana, USA
Wen-Hsing Lai, National Kaohsiung First University of Science and Technology, Taiwan
Zhihua Lai, Ranplan Wireless Network Design Ltd., UK
Jong-Hyouk Lee, INRIA, France
Wolfgang Leister, Norsk Regnesentral, Norway
Elizabeth I. Leonard, Naval Research Laboratory - Washington DC, USA
Richard Li, Huawei Technologies, USA
Jia-Chin Lin, National Central University, Taiwan
Chi (Harold) Liu, IBM Research - China, China
Diogo Lobato Acatauassu Nunes, Federal University of Pará, Brazil
Andreas Loeffler, Friedrich-Alexander-University of Erlangen-Nuremberg, Germany
Michael D. Logothetis, University of Patras, Greece
Renata Lopes Rosa, University of São Paulo, Brazil
Hongli Luo, Indiana University Purdue University Fort Wayne, USA
Christian Maciocco, Intel Corporation, USA
Dario Maggiorini, University of Milano, Italy
Maryam Tayefeh Mahmoudi, Research Institute for ICT, Iran
Krešimir Malarić, University of Zagreb, Croatia
Zoubir Mammeri, IRIT - Paul Sabatier University - Toulouse, France
Herwig Mannaert, University of Antwerp, Belgium
Michael Massoth, University of Applied Sciences - Darmstadt, Germany
Adrian Matei, Orange Romania S.A, part of France Telecom Group, Romania
Natarajan Meghanathan, Jackson State University, USA
Emmanouel T. Michailidis, University of Piraeus, Greece
Ioannis D. Moscholios, University of Peloponnese, Greece
Djafar Mynbaev, City University of New York, USA
Pubudu N. Pathirana, Deakin University, Australia
Christopher Nguyen, Intel Corp., USA
Lim Nguyen, University of Nebraska-Lincoln, USA
Brian Niehöfer, TU Dortmund University, Germany
Serban Georgica Obreja, University Politehnica Bucharest, Romania
Peter Orosz, University of Debrecen, Hungary
Patrik Österberg, Mid Sweden University, Sweden

Harald Øverby, ITEM/NTNU, Norway
Tudor Palade, Technical University of Cluj-Napoca, Romania
Constantin Paleologu, University Politehnica of Bucharest, Romania
Stelios Papaharalabos, National Observatory of Athens, Greece
Gerard Parr, University of Ulster Coleraine, UK
Ling Pei, Finnish Geodetic Institute, Finland
Jun Peng, University of Texas - Pan American, USA
Cathryn Peoples, University of Ulster, UK
Dionysia Petraki, National Technical University of Athens, Greece
Dennis Pfisterer, University of Luebeck, Germany
Timothy Pham, Jet Propulsion Laboratory, California Institute of Technology, USA
Roger Pierre Fabris Hoefel, Federal University of Rio Grande do Sul (UFRGS), Brazil
Przemyslaw Pochec, University of New Brunswick, Canada
Anastasios Politis, Technological & Educational Institute of Serres, Greece
Adrian Popescu, Blekinge Institute of Technology, Sweden
Neeli R. Prasad, Aalborg University, Denmark
Dušan Radović, TES Electronic Solutions, Stuttgart, Germany
Victor Ramos, UAM Iztapalapa, Mexico
Gianluca Reali, Università degli Studi di Perugia, Italy
Eric Renault, Telecom SudParis, France
Leon Reznik, Rochester Institute of Technology, USA
Joel Rodrigues, Instituto de Telecomunicações / University of Beira Interior, Portugal
David Sánchez Rodríguez, University of Las Palmas de Gran Canaria (ULPGC), Spain
Panagiotis Sarigiannidis, University of Western Macedonia, Greece
Michael Sauer, Corning Incorporated, USA
Marialisa Scatà, University of Catania, Italy
Zary Segall, Chair Professor, Royal Institute of Technology, Sweden
Sergei Semenov, Broadcom, Finland
Sandra Sendra Compte, Polytechnic University of Valencia, Spain
Dimitrios Serpanos, University of Patras and ISI/RC Athena, Greece
Adão Silva, University of Aveiro / Institute of Telecommunications, Portugal
Pushpendra Bahadur Singh, MindTree Ltd, India
Mariusz Skrocki, Orange Labs Poland / Telekomunikacja Polska S.A., Poland
Leonel Sousa, INESC-ID/IST, TU-Lisbon, Portugal
Cristian Stanciu, University Politehnica of Bucharest, Romania
Liana Stanescu, University of Craiova, Romania
Cosmin Stoica Spahiu, University of Craiova, Romania
Young-Joo Suh, POSTECH (Pohang University of Science and Technology), Korea
Hailong Sun, Beihang University, China
Jani Suomalainen, VTT Technical Research Centre of Finland, Finland
Fatma Tansu, Eastern Mediterranean University, Cyprus
Ioan Toma, STI Innsbruck/University Innsbruck, Austria
Božo Tomas, HT Mostar, Bosnia and Herzegovina
Piotr Tyczka, ITTI Sp. z o.o., Poland
John Vardakas, University of Patras, Greece
Andreas Veglis, Aristotle University of Thessaloniki, Greece
Luís Veiga, Instituto Superior Técnico / INESC-ID Lisboa, Portugal
Calin Vladeanu, "Politehnica" University of Bucharest, Romania
Benno Volk, ETH Zurich, Switzerland
Krzysztof Walczak, Poznan University of Economics, Poland
Krzysztof Walkowiak, Wroclaw University of Technology, Poland
Yang Wang, Georgia State University, USA
Yean-Fu Wen, National Taipei University, Taiwan, R.O.C.

International Journal on Advances in Telecommunications
Volume 9, Numbers 3 & 4, 2016

CONTENTS

Performance Analysis of MIMO Satellite Communications Via Multiple Terrestrial Non-Regenerative Relay Nodes

Styliani Fassoi, Emmanouel T. Michailidis, and Athanasios G. Kanatas
Department of Digital Systems
School of Information and Communication Technologies
University of Piraeus
80 Karaoli & Dimitriou St., 18534, Piraeus, Greece
{sfassoi, emichail, kanatas}@unipi.gr

Abstract—**Multiple-input multiple-output (MIMO) satellite communication systems have received the attention of the research community over the last years. This paper proposes a downlink MIMO satellite-to-terrestrial (S2T) system aided by multiple amplify-and-forward (AF) terrestrial relay nodes. This system intends to provide robust, reliable, and efficient communication links and improve the spectral efficiency and the total capacity of the network. In particular, this paper mainly concentrates on investigating the performance of the proposed system and evaluating the bit-error-rate (BER) and the channel capacity. To model the satellite and terrestrial channel, the Loo and Rician statistical distributions are utilized, respectively. One major implementation difficulty of the MIMO technology is the signal separation (detection) problem at the receiving side of the communication link due to interference from multistream transmission. In this paper, the linear zero-forcing (ZF) and minimum mean square error (MMSE) multi-antenna signal detection techniques are employed. To improve the performance without significantly increasing the complexity, ordered successive interference cancellation (SIC) techniques are also exploited.**

Keywords-Amplify and forward (AF) relaying; multiple-input multiple-output (MIMO) systems; satellite communications; signal detection techiques

I. INTRODUCTION

As new requirements for access to comprehensive broadband and broadcast/multicast high-speed wireless communication services are emerged, satellite communications can play an important role in the evolution of current and future communication systems by providing global coverage and ubiquitous access [1], [2]. Satellite networks intend to substantially support terrestrial backhaul networks and provide uninterrupted radio coverage to fixed, portable, and mobile terrestrial receivers. The development of next-generation communication systems envisages the synergetic and seamless integration of heterogeneous terrestrial and satellite networks with different capabilities, providing voice, text and multimedia services. Hybrid satellite-terrestrial networks are a typical example of cooperation between different architectures.

For the terrestrial infrastructure, the multiple-input multiple-output (MIMO) architecture has fulfilled the growing demands for high data throughputs and enhanced link reliability [3]. In recent years, theoretical and experimental efforts have been also devoted by academia and space agencies to the investigation of the applicability of multiple-antenna techniques to satellite systems and the potential enhancements that can be achieved through spatial and/or polarization diversity [4], [5].

The advantages of MIMO technology can be combined with the features of cooperative diversity techniques via intermediate relays [1], [6]-[9], in order to improve the quality of service (QoS), extend the network range, and preserve the end-to-end communication between a source and a destination. The most usual and well-defined types of relaying are the non-regenerative relaying, e.g., amplify-and-forward (AF) relaying, and the regenerative relaying, e.g., decode-and-forward (DF) relaying. In the first type, the relay is a conventional repeater, which just amplifies the received signal and forwards it to the destination. In the second type, the relay has an active role being able to decode the received signal, perform baseband signal processing, and retransmit the signal to the final destination.

In [10], [11], the use of relaying in a single-antenna hybrid satellite-to-terrestrial (S2T) communication system was proposed, whereas the performance of a single-antenna hybrid S2T multi-relay cooperative system was analyzed in [12]. Besides, a MIMO S2T communication system with a single terrestrial relay was proposed in [13]. The benefits regarding the outage probability, the symbol-error-rate (SER) and the ergodic capacity of a S2T communication system with a single multi-antenna relay compared to a conventional single-antenna relay system was underlined in [14]. Indeed, research on multi-relay networks with MIMO-enabled nodes remains limited. A cooperative multi-relay MIMO system, where every terminal in the network is employed with multiple antennas was presented in [15]. However, this system does not consider the special characteristics of the satellite radio channel.

This paper investigates the performance of a downlink MIMO S2T communication system with multiple terrestrial relay nodes in terms of the bit-error-rate (BER) and the available channel capacity. To model the satellite channel, the Loo statistical distribution is used [16]. Besides, the terrestrial channel is modeled using the Rician distribution. Since the receiver often observes a linear superposition of separately transmitted information that cannot be easily separated, this paper utilizes the linear zero-forcing (ZF) [17] and the minimum mean square error (MMSE) [18] signal detection techniques, which are characterized by computational simplicity compared to non-linear techniques. Moreover, the ordered successive interference cancellation (SIC) techniques are employed to enhance the performance without significantly affect the complexity at the receiver [19].

The rest of the paper is organized as follows. Section II presents a MIMO multi-relay S2T system. In Section III, the satellite and terrestrial radio channels are statistically modeled using widely accepted statistical distributions. Section IV focuses on signal detection techniques. Results are provided in Section V. Finally, conclusions and future research perspectives are drawn in Section VI.

II. System Model of The Multiple-Input Multiple-Output Satellite-to-Terrestrial Multi-Relay Communication System

In this section, a downlink MIMO S2T communication system is considered, where R full-duplex (FD) AF terrestrial relays (R) are assigned to assist the source (S), i.e., the satellite, in forwarding its information to the destination (D), i.e., terrestrial station. Although half-duplex (HD) relaying offers interference-free transmission at the cost of inefficient resource utilization, FD relaying has received significant attention and many studies suggest that by allowing a certain amount of loop-interference (LI), improved performance can be harvested compared to HD relaying [20]. It is assumed the antennas at the relays are isolated and that perfect LI cancellation is feasible. It is also assumed that the direct link between source and destination is obstructed due to high attenuation. The communication system comprises R intermediate relay nodes equipped with M_r transmit and M_t transmit antennas, where $M_r = M_t$. Besides, N_t and N_r antennas are used at the source and the destination, respectively. Fig. 1 depicts the communication scenario, whereas Fig. 2 demonstrates the system model.

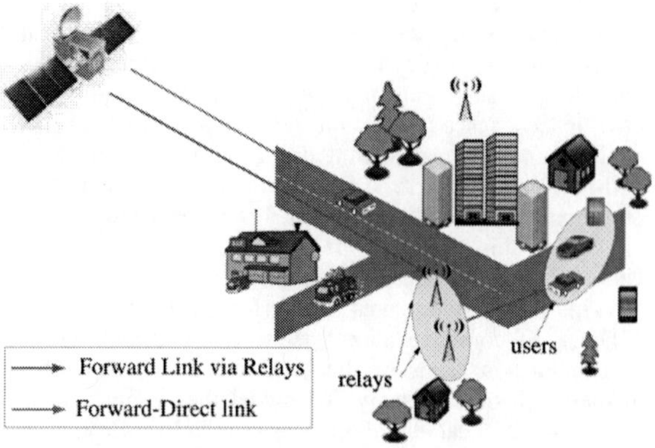

Figure 1. Simple representation of a multi-relay S2T system.

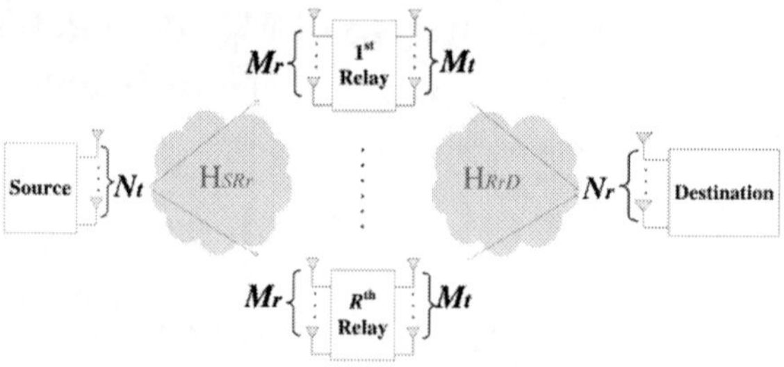

Figure 2. The system model of a MIMO multi-relay S2T system.

Note that the generalization to the case, where each relay has a distinct number of transmit and receive antennas can also be similarly incorporated in the following analysis but at the expense of a more complicated notation. The waves emitted from the source antennas travel over paths with different lengths and impinge the relays' antennas. Then, the relay nodes amplify and forward the received signal to the destination. The transmitted data consists of N_t independent data streams, which are allocated to the correspondingly numbered antennas at the source and relay nodes. The link between the source and the relays represents the satellite link, while the link between the relays and the destination can be modeled as a terrestrial link. Data are transmitted in N-symbol packets. All wireless radio channels are assumed uncorrelated, unless otherwise specified, with frequency-flat block fading, where the coherence time is equal to the duration of the N-symbol packet. Note that the entire system can be separated into $2R$ MIMO subsystems related with the communication link between the source and each relay, as well as each relay and the destination. It is considered that each relay processes the received signals independently.

First, the MIMO subsystem for the communication link between the source and the rth relay is considered. For this subsystem, the $M_r \times 1$ received signal at the rth relay for the ith symbol is given by

$$\mathbf{y}_{R_r}[i] = \mathbf{H}_{SR_r}[i]\mathbf{x}[i] + \mathbf{n}_{R_r}[i], \quad (1)$$

where the matrix $\mathbf{H}_{SR_r}$ is the rth $M_r \times N_t$ MIMO channel matrix (analytically presented in Section III), $\mathbf{x}$ is the $N_t \times 1$ input data vector satisfying $\mathbf{R}_x = E\left[\mathbf{x}\mathbf{x}^H\right]$, where $\mathrm{E}[\cdot]$ is the statistical expectation operator, and $(\cdot)^H$ denotes the complex conjugate (Hermitian) transpose operator, and $\mathbf{n}_{R_r}$ is the $M_r \times 1$ noise vector with additive white Gaussian noise (AWGN) at the rth relay's branches, whose variance is σ^2_{SRr}, the autocorrelation matrix is $\sigma^2_{SRr}\mathbf{I}_{SRr}$, and the covariance matrix is $\mathbf{R}_{nR_r} = E\left[\mathbf{n}_{R_r}\mathbf{n}^H_{R_r}\right]$. The signal received by all the relays can be expressed using an M_tR-element vector $\mathbf{y}_R[i]=\left[\mathbf{y}_{R_1}^T[i]\ \mathbf{y}_{R_2}^T[i]\ \cdots\ \mathbf{y}_{R_R}^T[i]\right]^T$ as follows [21]

$$\mathbf{y}_R[i]=\mathbf{H}_{SR}[i]\mathbf{x}[i]+\mathbf{n}_R[i], \tag{2}$$

where $\mathbf{H}_{SR}[i]=\left[\mathbf{H}_{SR_1}^T[i]\ \mathbf{H}_{SR_2}^T[i]\ \cdots\ \mathbf{H}_{SR_R}^T[i]\right]^T$ is the $M_tR\times N_t$ channel matrix between the source and the relays, and $\mathbf{n}_R$ is an $M_tR\times 1$ AWGN vector at the relays with $\mathbf{R}_{nR}=E\left[\mathbf{n}_R\mathbf{n}_R^H\right]$.

For the MIMO subsystem of the communication link between the rth relay and the destination, the $N_r\times 1$ received signal at the destination is the summation of the R relayed signals [15] and is given by

$$\mathbf{y}_D[i]=\sum_{r=1}^{R}a\mathbf{H}_{R_rD}[i]\mathbf{y}_{R_r}[i]+\mathbf{n}_D[i], \tag{3}$$

where a is the amplification factor, which is assumed identical for each relay branch, $\mathbf{H}_{R_rD}$ is the rth $N_r\times M_t$ MIMO channel matrix (analytically presented in Section III), $\mathbf{y}_{SR_i}$ is defined in (1), and $\mathbf{n}_D$ is the $N_r\times 1$ noise vector with AWGN at the destination's branches, whose variance is σ_{RrD}^2, and the autocorrelation matrix is $\sigma_{SRr}^2\mathbf{I}_{SRr}$, and the covariance matrix is $\mathbf{R}_{nd}=E\left[\mathbf{n}_D\mathbf{n}_D^H\right]$. The summation of (3) can be expressed in a more compact form as follows

$$\mathbf{y}_D[i]=a\mathbf{H}_{RD}[i]\mathbf{y}_R[i]+\mathbf{n}_D[i], \tag{4}$$

where $\mathbf{H}_{RD}[i]=\left[\mathbf{H}_{R_1D}[i]\ \mathbf{H}_{R_2D}[i]\ \cdots\ \mathbf{H}_{R_RD}[i]\right]$ is the $N_r\times M_tR$ compound channel matrix. The end-to-end signal-to-noise ratio (SNR) of each relay branch can be constructed from the compounded channels of the proposed system, as shown in [15, eq. (53)].

An important prospective feature of multi-relay MIMO communication networks is an increase in the channel capacity. The ergodic channel capacity (in bits/sec/Hz) of a MIMO AF multi-relay system is defined as the expectation of the instantaneous mutual information (MI) between the source and destination. Fundamentally, the MI is given by the difference between the differential entropy and the conditional differential entropy of the received signal at the destination via the relays when the transmit data are known. This can be expressed as [15]

$$I_d(\mathbf{x};\mathbf{y}_D)=H(\mathbf{y}_D)-H(\mathbf{y}_D\,|\,\mathbf{x}). \tag{5}$$

After extensive manipulations presented in [22] and [23], it is obtained that

$$I_d(\mathbf{x};\mathbf{y}_D)=\log_2\det\left(\mathbf{I}_{N_t}+E\left[a\mathbf{H}_{RD}[i]\mathbf{y}_R[i]\mathbf{y}_R^H[i]\mathbf{H}_{RD}^H\right]\right) \tag{6}$$

III. STATISTICAL MODELING OF THE SATELLITE AND TERRESTRIAL CHANNEL

The modeling of the satellite channel can be performed via a deterministic or statistical approach. Although the deterministic channel models are accurate, their computational complexity is large. In particular, the application of the deterministic channel models to satellite systems is not practically attractive, since a single satellite beam covers a wide propagation area and the determination of all the relevant paths between the satellite and the terrestrial station is difficult. On the contrary, the statistical channel models express the distribution of the received signal by means of the first-order statistics, such as the probability density function (PDF) or the cumulative distribution function (CDF), and the second-order statistics, such the level crossing rate (LCR) and the average fade duration (AFD). Since multipath and shadowing effects are important in the signal propagation, the statistical models usually assume that the received signal consists of two components, the line-of-sight (LoS) component and the non-line-of-sight (NLoS) component. Then, the relative power of the direct, i.e., LoS, and multipath, i.e., NLoS, components of the received signal is controlled by the Rician factor and the distributions of these two components are usually studied separately.

The statistical models for S2T channels can be characterized into two categories; single state and multi-state models [24]. The single state channel models are described by single statistical distributions and can be used fixed satellite scenarios, where the channel statistics remain constant over the areas of interest. Besides, the multi-state channel models are used for non-stationary time-varying propagation conditions.

In this section, a single-state statistical modeling approach for the satellite and the terrestrial channel is described. Specifically, the satellite channel is modeled using the Loo distribution [16], where the long-term shadowing due to roadside trees affects only the LoS component and is described through a log-normal distribution, whereas the NLoS component is described by a Rayleigh PDF. Hence, the resulting complex signal envelope is the sum of correlated lognormal and Rayleigh processes. The Loo distribution assumes that the foliage not only attenuates but also scatters the radio waves. In addition, the Rician distribution is utilized, in order to model the terrestrial channel. Then, a strong LoS signal also arrives at the receiver branches and the fading envelope follows a Rice distribution.

A. Modeling of the satellite radio channel

As previously mentioned, for the communication link between the satellite and the terrestrial relays, the Loo distribution is used, which was verified experimentally by conducting measurements in rural areas with elevation angles up to 30° [25]. Using the Loo distribution, the channel matrix of the satellite link for the envelope h_{ij} is given by

$$\mathbf{H}_{SR_r} = \left[h_{ij}\right] = \left[\overline{h_{ij}}\right] + \left[\widetilde{h_{ij}}\right] = \overline{\mathbf{H}}_{SR_r} + \widetilde{\mathbf{H}}_{SR_r}, \quad (7)$$

where

$$\begin{aligned} h_{ij} &= \left|h_{ij}\right| \exp\left(j\phi_{i,j}\right) \\ &= \left|\overline{h_{ij}}\right| \exp\left(j\overline{\phi_{i,j}}\right) + \left|\widetilde{h_{ij}}\right| \exp\left(j\widetilde{\phi_{i,j}}\right) \end{aligned} \quad (8)$$

and $\overline{\phi_{i,j}}$, $\widetilde{\phi_{i,j}}$ are uniformly distributed over $[0, 2\pi]$. The first factor represents the log-normal fading, while the second one describes the Rayleigh fading. Therefore, the Loo distribution extracted from (8) is the superposition of the log-normal distribution to model the large-scale fading and Rayleigh distribution for the modeling of small-scale fading. Specifically, the Loo probability density function is given by

$$p\left(\left|h_{ij}\right|\right) = \frac{\left|h_{ij}\right|}{b_0\sqrt{2\pi\sigma^2}} \times \int_0^\infty \frac{1}{\overline{h}_{ij}} \exp\left[-\frac{\left(\ln \overline{h}_{ij} - \mu\right)^2}{2\sigma^2} - \frac{\left|\overline{h}_{ij}\right|^2 + \overline{h}_{ij}^2}{2b_0}\right] I_0\left(\frac{\left|h_{ij}\right|\overline{h}_{ij}}{b_0}\right) d\overline{h}_{ij} \quad (9)$$

where b_0 is the average scattered power resulting from the multipath components, σ and μ are the standard deviation and mean, respectively, and $I_0(\cdot)$ is the zero order modified Bessel function of the first kind.

B. Modeling of the terrestrial radio channel

The terrestrial wireless radio channel is mostly characterized by the surrounding local scatterers in the vicinity of the terrestrial nodes, which produce multipath components. Since a strong LoS component is also present, the propagation environment can be characterized using the Rician distribution as follows [26]

$$\mathbf{H}_{R_r D} = \sqrt{\frac{K_r}{K_r + 1}} \overline{\mathbf{H}}_{R_r D} + \sqrt{\frac{1}{K_r + 1}} \widetilde{\mathbf{H}}_{R_r D}, \quad (10)$$

where K_r is the Rician factor, which expresses the relative power of the direct and scattered components of the received signal for the link between the rth relay and the destination and provides an indication of the link quality, $\overline{\mathbf{H}}_{R_r D}$ is a deterministic unit rank matrix, which represents the direct component, and $\widetilde{\mathbf{H}}_{R_r D}$ is the channel matrix of the multipath components. When $K_r = 0$ the channel is described by a Rayleigh distribution, whereas a very large value of K_r, i.e., $K_r \to \infty$, implies the presence of a Gaussian channel.

Recent studies have shown that the performance of MIMO systems strongly depends on the Rician factor [27]. In particular, as the Rician factor increases, the correlation between MIMO subchannels also increases [28]. Hence, efficient and accurate methods for estimating the Rician factor are of considerable interest [29]. Several values of the Rician factor have been reported in the literature from measurement campaigns and studies performed in the L- and S- frequency bands for satellite communications systems [30]. According to these measurements, the value of the Rician factor depends on the elevation angle of the satellite and the operating frequency. Nevertheless, the value of the Rician factor also depends on the propagation area, and the degree of urbanization. Thus, the Rician factor is expected to be lower in highly urbanized areas, where the scatterers are usually dense.

IV. Linear Signal Detection Schemes

In MIMO systems, spatial multiplexing is exploited, where multiple streams of independent data are transmitted from the transmitting antennas. These streams should be then separated at the receiver by means of appropriate processing techniques. Hence, signal detection is required for the signals. In this paper, standard linear signal detection methods for MIMO spatial multiplexing systems are used due to their simplicity, versatility, well-understood characteristics, and ease of extracting performance metrics. In linear signal detectors, a linear transform is applied to the outputs of conventional matched filters to produce a new set of outputs, which may generate better results. These detectors treat all transmitted signals as interferences except for the desired stream from the target antenna at the transmitter. Therefore, interference signals from other antennas are minimized or nullified in the course of detecting the desired signal from the target antenna. To facilitate the detection of signals from each antenna, the estimated symbols are inverted by a weight matrix $\mathbf{W}$ as follows [22]

$$\tilde{\mathbf{x}} = \left[\tilde{x}_1 \tilde{x}_2 \cdots \tilde{x}_{N_t}\right]^T = \mathbf{W}\mathbf{y}, \quad (11)$$

where $\mathbf{y} = \mathbf{H}\mathbf{x} + \mathbf{n}$ is the receive vector, $\mathbf{H}$ is the channel matrix, $\mathbf{x}$ is the transmit vector, and $\mathbf{n}$ is the noise vector for a generic MIMO communication system. Hence, a linear combination of the received signals in the destination node is considered. Note that there is one detection for each symbol, which depends on the number of the transmit antennas. The standard linear detection methods include the well-defined and widely used ZF and MMSE linear signal detection techniques.

The simplest MIMO detector is the ZF detector, which simply inverts the channel matrix and attempts to completely remove (forced to zero) the interference caused by the channel. For the case when the inverse of the channel does not exist, the pseudoinverse of the channel matrix is used. The ZF detection technique assumes that the base station has perfect knowledge of the channel state information (CSI) of all users' equipment present at the receiver.

The weight matrix of the ZF technique is given by [22]

$$\mathbf{W}_{ZF} = \left(\mathbf{H}^H\mathbf{H}\right)^{-1}\mathbf{H}^H, \tag{12}$$

where $(\cdot)^H$ is the Hermitian transpose operation. Thus, we obtain

$$\begin{aligned}\tilde{\mathbf{x}}_{ZF} &= \mathbf{W}_{ZF}\mathbf{y}\\ &= \left(\mathbf{H}^H\mathbf{H}\right)^{-1}\mathbf{H}^H(\mathbf{Hx}+\mathbf{n})\\ &= \underbrace{\left(\mathbf{H}^H\mathbf{H}\right)^{-1}\mathbf{H}^H\mathbf{H}}_{1}\mathbf{x}+\left(\mathbf{H}^H\mathbf{H}\right)^{-1}\mathbf{H}^H\mathbf{n}\\ &= \mathbf{x}+\left(\mathbf{H}^H\mathbf{H}\right)^{-1}\mathbf{H}^H\mathbf{n}.\\ &= \mathbf{x}+\tilde{\mathbf{n}}_{ZF},\end{aligned} \tag{13}$$

where $\tilde{\mathbf{n}}_{ZF} = \left(\mathbf{H}^H\mathbf{H}\right)^{-1}\mathbf{H}^H\mathbf{n}$. Note that the ZF detector performs poorly when the channel matrix is close to being singular, since it amplifies the noise. On the other hand, when the channel matrix is orthogonal, this suboptimal linear detector does not amplify the noise, and is equivalent to a decision feedback or non-linear maximum likelihood (ML) detector [31]. The latter is considered as an optimal complex technique in the sense of minimum error probability, when all data vectors are equally likely, and it fully exploits the available diversity.

The noise enhancement effect plaguing the ZF detection technique can be reduced by using the MMSE detection technique, which is also considered suboptimal. To maximize the post-detection signal to interference plus noise ratio (SINR), the MMSE weight matrix is given by [22]

$$\mathbf{W}_{MMSE} = \left(\mathbf{H}^H\mathbf{H}+\sigma^2\mathbf{I}\right)^{-1}\mathbf{H}^H. \tag{14}$$

The MMSE receiver uses the statistical information of noise σ^2. Thus, using the MMSE weight in (11), we obtain

$$\begin{aligned}\tilde{\mathbf{x}}_{MMSE} &= \mathbf{W}_{MMSE}\mathbf{y}_2\\ &= \left(\mathbf{H}^H\mathbf{H}+\sigma^2\mathbf{I}\right)^{-1}\mathbf{H}^H(\mathbf{Hx}+\mathbf{n})\\ &= \underbrace{\left(\mathbf{H}^H\mathbf{H}+\sigma^2\mathbf{I}\right)^{-1}\mathbf{H}^H\mathbf{H}}_{1}\mathbf{x}+\left(\mathbf{H}^H\mathbf{H}+\sigma^2\mathbf{I}\right)^{-1}\mathbf{H}^H\mathbf{n}\\ &= \mathbf{x}+\left(\mathbf{H}^H\mathbf{H}+\sigma^2\mathbf{I}\right)^{-1}\mathbf{H}^H\mathbf{n}.\\ &= \mathbf{x}+\tilde{\mathbf{n}}_{MMSE},\end{aligned} \tag{15}$$

where $\tilde{\mathbf{n}}_{MMSE} = \left(\mathbf{H}^H\mathbf{H}+\sigma^2\mathbf{I}\right)^{-1}\mathbf{H}^H\mathbf{n}$.

Although non-linear reception offers performance advantages in MIMO systems by assisting in the mitigation of the multi-antenna interference, the linear detection methods are characterized by low complexity in terms of hardware implementation. To improve their performance without significantly increasing their complexity associated with other non-linear methods, ordered SIC techniques can be exploited. These techniques consider a bank of linear receivers, each of which detects one of the parallel data streams, such that the detected signal components successively canceled from the received signal at each stage. The signal is first obtained in the detection step of each propagation path signal. Then, the signals are combined to detect each substream. More specifically, the detected signal in each stage is subtracted from the received signal so that the remaining signal with the reduced interference can be used in the subsequent stage [22].

Fig. 3 illustrates the ordered SIC signal detection process for four spatial streams, i.e., N_t = 4. Let us denote x_i the symbol to be detected in the ith order, which may be different from the transmit signal at the ith antenna, since $x_{(i)}$ depends on the order of detection. Let $\tilde{x}_{(i)}$ denote a sliced value of $x_{(i)}$. In ordered SIC techniques, symbol estimation can be obtained using a linear detector, such as ZF or MMSE. The first stream is estimated with the first row vector of the ZF and MMSE weight matrix in (13) and (15), respectively.

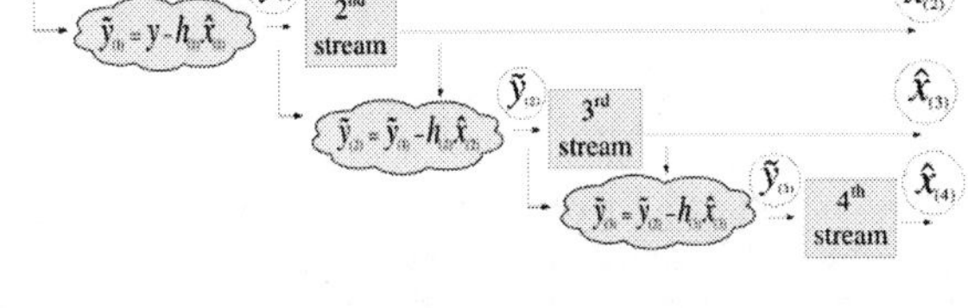

Figure 3. Illustration of the ordered SIC signal detection for four spatial streams.

Providing that $x_{(1)} = \hat{x}_{(1)}$, the interference is successfully canceled in the course of estimating $x_{(2)}$. However, if $x_{(1)} \neq \hat{x}_{(1)}$, error propagation is incurred, since the MMSE weight, which was designed under the precondition of the equality $x_{(1)} = \hat{x}_{(1)}$, is used for the estimation of $x_{(2)}$. Due to the error propagation caused by erroneous decision in the previous stages, the order of detection has significant influence on the performance of ordered SIC detection. For the SIC-ZF technique, we obtain

$$\tilde{\mathbf{x}}_{SIC-ZF} = \mathbf{W}_{ZF}\tilde{\mathbf{y}}_i, \quad (16)$$

where $\tilde{\mathbf{y}}_i = \mathbf{y}_D - h_i\tilde{\mathbf{x}}_{ZF}$ for the ith stream estimation. Similarly, for the SIC-MMSE technique, we also obtain

$$\tilde{\mathbf{x}}_{SIC-MMSE} = \mathbf{W}_{MMSE}\tilde{\mathbf{y}}_i, \quad (17)$$

where $\tilde{\mathbf{y}}_i = \mathbf{y}_D - h_i\tilde{\mathbf{x}}_{MMSE}$ for the ith stream estimation.

This paper considers an AF DF multi-relay MIMO system. However, in a more realistic scenario, the capacity of a MIMO channel using a linear detector is given by

$$C_{LD} = \sum_{i=1}^{k} \log_2\left(1 + SINR_k\right), \quad (18)$$

where the $SINR_k$ for each receiver is different. The SINR for the MMSE receiver for the kth spatial stream can be expressed as [32]

$$SINR_k^{MMSE} = \frac{1}{\left[\left(\mathbf{I}_{Nt} + SNR * \mathbf{H}^H (\mathbf{R}_n)^{-1}\mathbf{H}\right)^{-1}\right]_{kk}} - 1, \quad (19)$$

where $\mathbf{I}_{Nt}$ is a $N_t \times N_t$ identity matrix and $\mathbf{H}^H$ is the Hermitian transpose of $\mathbf{H}$. The SINR for the ZF receiver denoted by $SINR_k^{ZF}$ can be expressed as follows by conditioning on $\mathbf{H}$ [17]

$$SINR_k^{ZF} = \frac{SNR}{\left[\left(\mathbf{H}^H (\mathbf{R}_n)^{-1}\mathbf{H}\right)^{-1}\right]_{kk}}. \quad (20)$$

V. RESULTS

This section demonstrates the performance of the proposed communication system with reference to the BER and the available channel capacity. To investigate the performance of the MIMO multi-relay S2T system, two scenarios are initially examined (see Fig. 4). In the first scenario, a single-relay system is considered with two antennas at the source, relay, and destination. The second scenario includes two synchronized relay nodes each equipped with single antennas. For the first scenario, the Rician factor is set to 10 dB, whereas for the second scenario, the Rician factor is set to 8 dB for the communication link between the source and the first relay and 10 dB for the communication link between the source and the second relay, respectively.

Fig. 5 demonstrates the end-to-end BER performance for the aforementioned two communication scenarios. QPSK modulation is used, since satellite communications are sensitive to data loss due to the limited resources. According to the results, the best performance is achieved with SIC-MMSE, while the worst with ZF for both scenarios. In addition, the MIMO two-relay S2T system outperforms the MIMO single-relay S2T system.

In Fig. 6, the advantage of the MMSE technique over the ZF technique is depicted in terms of the channel capacity. However, this advantage is nullified as the SNR increases.

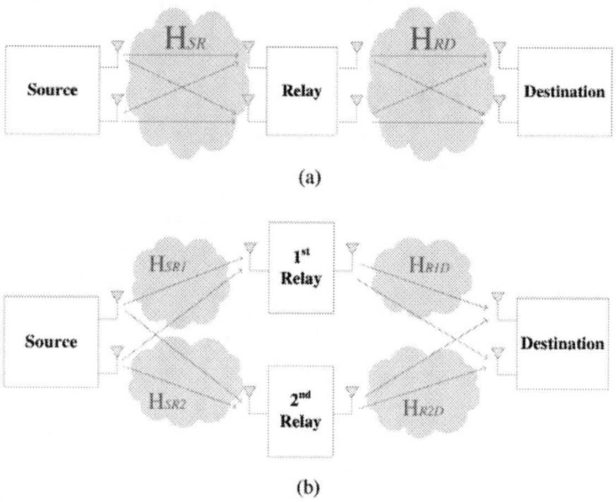

Figure 4. (a) A MIMO single-relay S2T communication system (b) A MIMO two-relay S2T communication system.

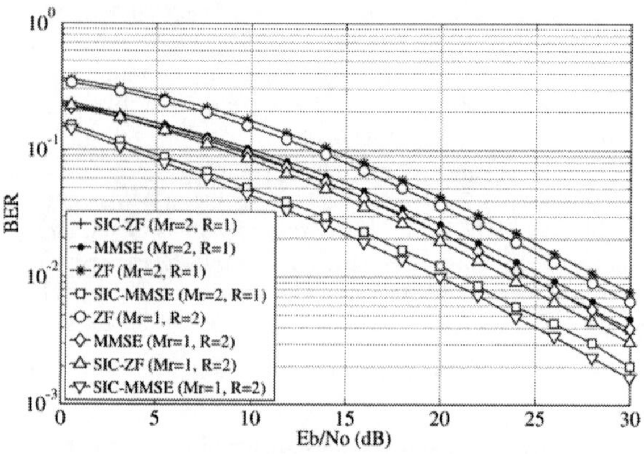

Figure 5. End-to-end BER performance of a MIMO S2T communication system, where a single relay equipped with two antennas or two relays equipped with single antennas are used.

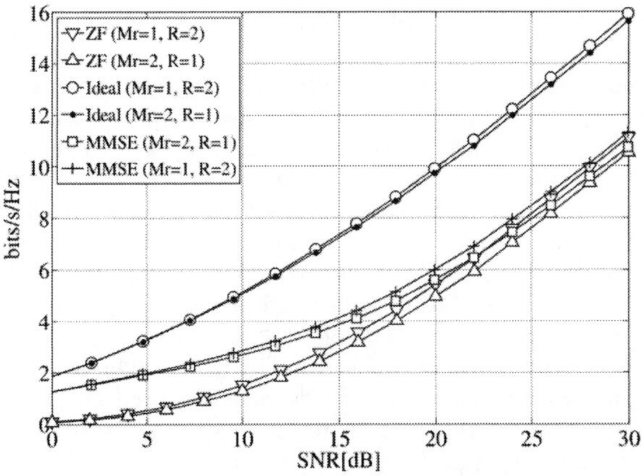

Figure 6. Channel capacity of a MIMO S2T communication system, where a single relay equipped with two antennas or two relays equipped with single antennas are used.

In Fig. 7, different propagation scenarios are examined regarding the BER for a MIMO single-relay S2T system. Specifically, the Loo-Rician, Loo-Rayleigh, Rician-Rician, and Rician-Rayleigh distributions are compared. ZF signal detection is exploited and it is considered that the source, the destination, and the relay are equipped with two antennas. One observes that the performance is better, as soon as the Loo-Rayleigh fading distribution is considered, i.e., the Loo distribution is used for the link between source and relay, whereas the Rayleigh distribution is used for the link between relay and destination.

The effect of the Rician factor, which controls the strength of the LoS component is demonstrated in Fig. 8, where identical values of the Rician factor are used for the different links. In particular, the BER performance degrades as the Rician factor increases. Overall, the results in Figs. 7 and 8 confirm that the MIMO advantages can be successfully exploited in propagation environments, which are characterized by a sufficiently large number of non-coherent diffuse components.

In Fig. 9, the effect of the value of the amplification factor on the end-to-end BER performance of a MIMO S2T communication system is illustrated, where a single relay equipped with two antennas and SIC-MMSE techniques are used. One observes that increasing the amplification factor improves the performance.

Fig. 10 shows the end-to-end BER performance of a MIMO single-relay S2T communication system for different digital modulation schemes, i.e., BPSK, QPSK, 8-PSK, and 16-PSK. It is clear that BPSK is the preferred modulation scheme for the proposed system.

Fig. 11 demonstrates the channel capacity as a function of the number of relays and the number of antennas at the relays. The capacity increases as the number of single-antenna relays increases. However, when the relays are equipped with a large number of antennas, increasing the number of relays has an insignificant effect on the capacity.

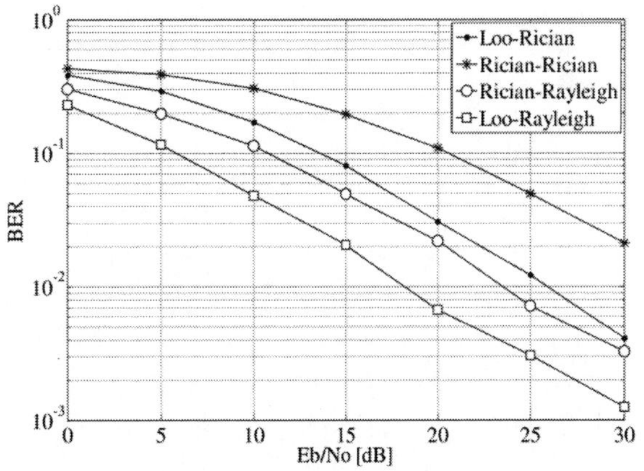

Figure 7. End-to-end BER performance of a MIMO single-relay S2T communication system for different statistical modeling of the satellite and terrestrial channel.

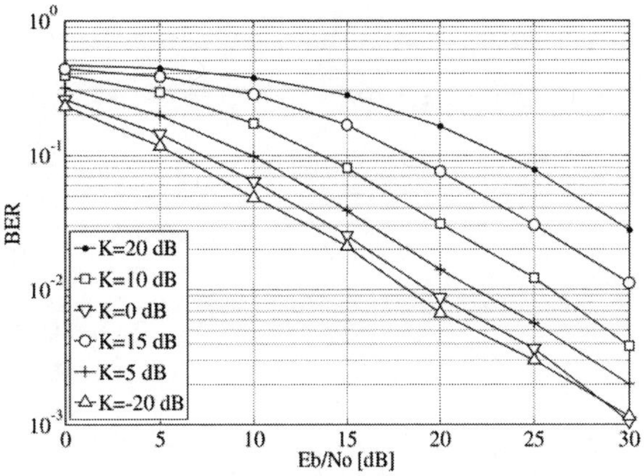

Figure 8. End-to-end BER performance in terms of the Rician factor of a MIMO S2T communication system, where a single relay equipped with two antennas and SIC-MMSE techniques are used.

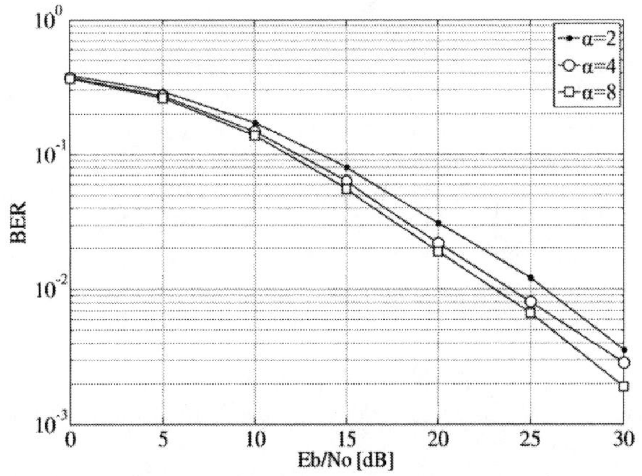

Figure 9. End-to-end BER performance in terms of the amplification factor of a MIMO S2T communication system, where a single relay equipped with two antennas and SIC-MMSE techniques are used.

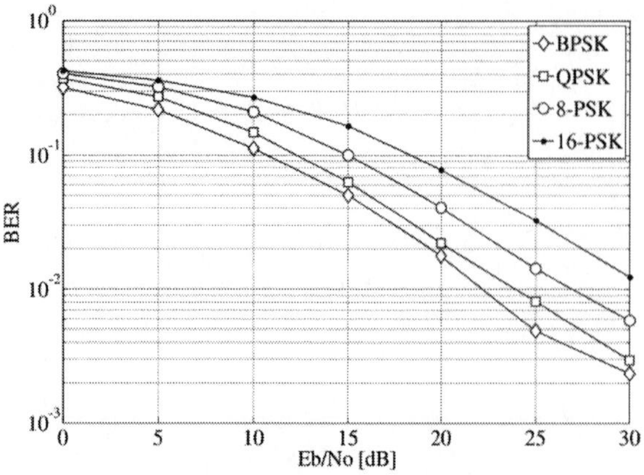

Figure 10. End-to-end BER performance of a MIMO S2T communication system, where a single relay equipped with two antennas and different digital modulation techniques are used.

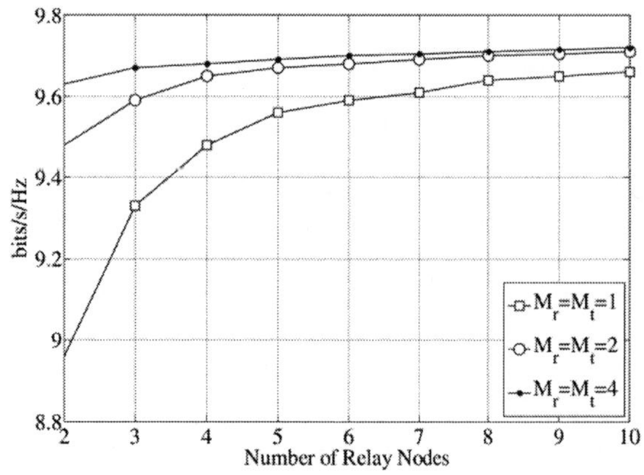

Figure 11. Channel capacity of a MIMO S2T communication system for different number of relays and different number of antennas at the relays.

VI. CONCLUSION AND FUTURE WORK

In this paper, the benefits of using multiple antenna techniques in relay-based S2T systems have been demonstrated. Specifically, the performance of a MIMO S2T communications via single or multiple AF relays for the forward link has been investigated. The results have shown the gain in the BER and the achievable channel capacity by applying ZF, MMSE, SIC-ZF, SIC-MMSE signal detection schemes in different propagation conditions. These results have also underlined that the most promising system model for future reliable wireless networks in difficult terrains and/or high distances is the one that uses BPSK modulation and SIC-MMSE signal detectors.

Nevertheless, this work could be further improved or extended into different areas. Due to the lack of channel-sounding measurement campaigns, the contribution of this work has been limited to theoretical results. However, it is important to verify this results in real-world propagation conditions. Moreover, other relaying techniques, such as DF relaying, and more sophisticated signal detection techniques, such as the non-linear ML and Tomlinson-Harashima Precoding (THP) techniques, may be exploited, in order to involve additional signal processing and improve error rate performance. The direct link from the source to the destination could be also considered in addition to the indirect source to destination link via the relay nodes, in order to construct a cooperative communication system and test its performance. Finally, multi-beam techniques based on the sufficient spatial separation of the users on ground and proper partitioning of the coverage area can be also exploited, in order to further increase the spectral efficiency of MIMO S2T multi-relay systems.

REFERENCES

[1] S. Fassoi, D. Christopoulos, S. Chatzinotas, E. T. Michailidis, A. G. Kanatas, and B. Ottersten, "Terrestrial to Satellite Communications Using Multi-antenna Relays Nodes," in *Proc. 7th International Conference on Advances in Satellite and Space Communications (SPACOMM) 2015*, Barcelona, Spain, pp. 46-51, 19-24 Apr. 2015.

[2] B. Evans, M. Werner, E. Lutz, M. Bousquet, G. E. Corazza, G. Maral, and R. Rumeau, "Integration of Satellite and Terrestrial Systems in Future Multimedia Communications," *IEEE Wireless Communications*, vol. 12, no. 5, pp. 72-80, Oct. 2005.

[3] A. J. Paulraj, D. A. Gore, R. U. Nabar, and H. Bolcskei, "An Overview of MIMO Communications – A Key to Gigabit Wireless," *Proceedings of the IEEE*, vol. 92, no. 2, pp. 198-218, Feb. 2004.

[4] P.-D. Arapoglou, K. Liolis, M. Bertinelli, A. Panagopoulos, P. Cottis, and R. De Gaudenzi, "MIMO over Satellite: A Review," *IEEE Communications Surveys & Tutorials*, vol. 13, no. 1, pp. 27-51, First Quarter 2011.

[5] P.-D. Arapoglou, E. T. Michailidis, A. D. Panagopoulos, A. G. Kanatas, and R. Prieto-Cerdeira, "The Land Mobile Earth-Space Channel: SISO to MIMO Modeling from L- to Ka- Bands," *IEEE Vehicular Technology Magazine*, vol. 6, no. 2, pp. 44-53, Jun. 2011.

[6] A. Nosratinia, T. E. Hunter, and A. Hedayat, "Cooperative communication in wireless networks," *IEEE Commun. Mag.*, vol. 42, no. 10, pp. 74-80, Oct. 2004.

[7] R. U. Nabar, H. Bölcskei, and F. W. Kneubuhler, "Fading relay channels: Performance limits and space-time signal design," *IEEE J. Sel. Areas Commun.*, vol. 22, no. 6, pp. 1099-1109, Aug. 2004.

[8] B. Paillassa, B. Escrig, R. Dhaou, R., M.-L. Boucheret, and C. Bes, "Improving satellite services with cooperative communications," *Int. J. Satell. Commun. Network.*, vol. 29, no. 6, pp. 479-500, Nov./Dec. 2011.

[9] Y. Fan and J. Thompson, "MIMO Configurations for Relay Channels: Theory and Practice," *IEEE Trans. on Wireless Communications*, vol. 6, no. 5, pp. 1774-1786, May 2007.

[10] M. K. Arti, "Channel Estimation and Detection in Hybrid Satellite–Terrestrial Communication Systems," *IEEE Trans. on Vehicular Technology*, vol. 65, no. 7, pp. 5764-5771, Jul. 2016.

[11] V. K. Sakarellos, C. Kourogiorgas, and A. D. Panagopoulos, "Cooperative hybrid land mobile satellite–terrestrial broadcasting systems: Outage probability evaluation and accurate simulation," *Wirel. Pers. Communic.*, vol. 79, no. 2, pp. 1471-1481, Nov. 2014.

[12] Y. Bu, M. Lin, K. An, et al., "Performance Analysis of Hybrid Satellite–Terrestrial Cooperative Systems with Fixed Gain Relaying," *Wirel. Pers. Communic.*, vol. 89, no. 2, pp. 427-445, Jul. 2016.

[13] Y. Dhungana, N. Rajatheva and C. Tellambura, "Performance Analysis of Antenna Correlation on LMS-Based Dual-Hop AF MIMO Systems," *IEEE Trans. on Vehicular Technology*, vol. 61, no. 8, pp. 3590-3602, Oct. 2012.

[14] A. Iqbal and K. M. Ahmed, "Impact of MIMO enabled relay on the performance of a hybrid satellite-terrestrial system," *Telecommun Syst.*, vol. 58, no. 1, pp. 17-31, Jan. 2015.
[15] P. Clarke and R. C. de Lamare, "Transmit Diversity and Relay Selection Algorithms for Multirelay Cooperative MIMO Systems," *IEEE Trans. on Vehicular Technology*, vol. 61, no. 3, pp. 1084-1098, Mar. 2012.
[16] C. Loo, "A statistical model for a land mobile satellite link," *IEEE Transactions on Vehicular Technology*, vol. 34, no. 3, pp. 122-127, 1985.
[17] R. Xu, F.C.M. Lau, "Performance analysis for MIMO systems using zero forcing detector over fading channels," *Communications, IEE Proceedings*, vol. 153, no. 1, pp.74-80, 2 Feb. 2006.
[18] D. Christopoulos, J. Arnau, S. Chatzinotas, C. Mosquera, and B. Ottersten, "MMSE performance analysis of generalized multibeam satellite channels," *Communications Letters, IEEE* , vol. 17, no. 7, pp. 1332–1335, 2013.
[19] M. Mandloi and V. Bhatia, "Ordered iterative successive interference cancellation algorithm for large MIMO detection," in *Proc. IEEE International Conference on Signal Processing, Informatics, Communication and Energy Systems (SPICES) 2015*, Kochi, Kerala, India, pp. 1-5, 19 - 21 Feb. 2015.
[20] I. Krikidis, H. A. Suraweera, P. J. Smith and Chau Yuen, "Full-duplex relay selection for amplify-and-forward cooperative networks," *IEEE Trans. Wirel. Commun.*, vol. 11, no.12, pp. 4381-4393, Dec. 2012.
[21] Y. Fu, L. Yang and W. P. Zhu, "A nearly optimal amplify-and-forward relaying scheme for two-hop MIMO multi-relay networks," *IEEE Communications Letters*, vol. 14, no. 3, pp. 229-231, Mar. 2010.
[22] Y. S. Cho, J. Kim, W. Y. Yang, and C. G. Kang, *MIMO-OFDM Wireless Communications with Matlab*, Wiley, 2010.
[23] I. Telatar, "Capacity of multi-antenna Gaussian channels," *Eur. Trans. Telecommun.*, vol. 10, no. 6, pp. 585–595, Nov. 1999.
[24] A. Abdi, W.C. Lau, M.-S. Alouini, M. Kaveh, "A new simple model for land mobile satellite channels: First- and second-order statistics," *IEEE Trans. Wireless Commun.*, vol. 2, no. 3, pp. 519-528, 2003.
[25] C. Loo and J. S. Butterworth, "Land mobile satellite channel measurements and modeling," in *Proceedings of the IEEE*, vol. 86, no. 7, pp. 1442-1463, Jul. 1998.
[26] N. Letzepis and A. Grant, "Capacity of the multiple spot beam satellite channel with Rician fading," *IEEE Trans. Inf. Theory*, vol. 54, no. 11, pp. 5210-5222, Nov. 2008.
[27] V. Tarokh, N. Seshadri, and A. R. Calderbank, "Space-time codes for high data rate wireless communication: Performance criterion and code construction," *IEEE Trans. on Information Theory*, vol. 44, no. 2, pp. 744-765, Mar. 1998.
[28] A. Abdi and M. Kaveh, "A space-time correlation model for multielement antenna systems in mobile fading channels," *IEEE Journal on Selec. Areas in Commun.*, vol. 20, no. 3, pp. 550-560, Apr. 2002.
[29] A. Abdi, C. Tepedelenlioglu, M. Kaveh, and G. Giannakis, "On the estimation of the K parameter for the Rice fading distribution," *IEEE Commun. Letters*, vol. 5, no. 3, pp. 92-94, Mar. 2001.
[30] A. Jahn, "Propagation considerations and fading countermeasures for mobile multimedia services," *Int. Journal on Satellite Commun.*, vol. 19, no. 3, pp. 223-250, 2001.
[31] W. Peng, S. Ma, T. S. Ng, and J. Wang, "A novel analytical method for maximum likelihood detection in MIMO multiplexing systems," *IEEE Trans. on Communications*, vol. 57, no. 8, pp. 2264-2268, Aug. 2009.
[32] M. Jing, Z. Ying, S. Xin, and Y. Yan, "On capacity of wireless ad hoc networks with MIMO MMSE receivers," *IEEE Trans. on Wireless Communications*, vol. 7, no. 12, pp. 5493-5503, Dec. 2008.

Analysis of the Optimum Switching Points in an Adaptive Modulation System in a Nakagami-*m* Fading Channel Considering Throughput and Delay Criteria

Ana Paula Teles Ribeiro da Silva and José Marcos Câmara Brito
Instituto Nacional de Telecomunicações - INATEL
Santa Rita do Sapucaí, Brazil
e-mail:anaptrs@gmail.com, brito@inatel.br

Abstract— **The adaptive modulation technique is a promising solution to resolve the problem of spectrum scarcity. A key issue that defines the performance of adaptive modulation systems is the ability to find the optimum switching points between neighboring modulations. In this paper, we analyze the influence of the fading channel model in the optimum switching points, assuming a Nakagami-*m* fading model and both real and non-real-time traffic. Therefore, two criteria were considered to determine the optimum switching points: the maximum throughput criterion, for a real-time traffic scenario, and the delay criterion, for a non-real-time traffic scenario.**

Keywords- Adaptive modulation; delay criterion; maximum throughput criterion; Nakagami-m fading; optimum switching points.

I. INTRODUCTION

Due to the exponential growing of the traffic in telecommunications networks in the last years, problems like the demand for higher transmission rates and the scarcity of spectrum have become extremely relevant. Several studies have been developed in order to improve the performance and ensure Quality of Service (QoS) for such networks. In this regard, the adaptive modulation technique has gained great attention as a promising solution to improve the performance of channels with time-varying conditions. For example, reference [1], published in ICN 2016, analyses the optimum switching point in an adaptive modulation system in a particular scenario.

Adaptive modulation technique consists of the dynamic adaptation of the modulation scheme as a function of the channel's state, according to a given performance criterion. The receiver makes an estimation of the channel state and sends this information back to the transmitter through a feedback channel. Based on this information, the transmitter modifies the modulation order, so that it better matches the conditions of the channel at that time [1] – [6].

The definition of the best points to switch between two modulations is a key issue in the adaptive modulation technique. In general, the change in modulation order occurs between neighboring modulations. Given a modulation with 2^n points in its constellation, the neighboring modulation has 2^{n-1} or 2^{n+1} points in its constellation [1] [4] [5].

Several ways of determining the switching points between neighboring modulations have been mentioned in the literature. The most common are to determine the switching points as a function of a target for the bit error rate (BER) [2] or a target for the packet error rate (PER) in the channel [6]. However, as proven in [4], these criteria do not optimize some QoS parameters, such as throughput and delay; thus, these authors proposed the calculation of the optimum switching points based on the maximum throughput criterion, considering real-time traffic, and the delay to transmit a correct PDU (Packet Data Unit) for non-real-time traffic. The analysis presented in [4] considers a memory-less channel, e.g., an AWGN (Additive White Gaussian Noise) channel in a wireless ATM (Asynchronous Transfer Mode) network. This approach, however, is not appropriate for several wireless channels, in which there is fading. Then, in [5], the authors extended the analysis presented in [4], taking into account Rayleigh fading channels. In [1], the authors extended the analysis presented in [4] and [5], considering a more general fading model: a Nakagami-*m* channel. However, in [1], the authors analyzed the influence of the channel model in the optimum switching points, taking into account only the maximum throughput criterion.

In this paper, we extended the analysis presented in [1] [4] [5], examining in depth the influence of the channel model in the optimum switching points of an adaptive modulation scheme and considering a Nakagami-*m* fading channel and two scenarios: real-time and non-real-time traffic. To compute the optimum switching points, we use the maximum throughput criterion for scenarios with real-time traffic and the delay criterion for non-real-time traffic, where a packet received with error can be retransmitted until it is correctly received.

The analysis in this paper considers transmissions in a wireless network with a Nakagami-*m* block fading channel that uses adaptive *M*-ary Quadrature Amplitude Modulation (*M*-QAM).

The remainder of this paper is organized as follows: In Section II, we introduce the system and channel models; in Section III, we present the calculation of the exact PER in the channel, which is necessary to compute the throughput and the delay. The maximum throughput criterion is presented in Section IV, and the delay criterion is discussed in Section V; Section VI presents the numerical results, and finally, we present our conclusions in Section VII.

II. System and Channel Models

In this section, we define the characteristics of the system and the channel model considered in this paper.

A. System Model

The system is composed of one base station, which manages all traffic, and several users that transmit over the wireless network, following the model presented in [4]. We assume a network using TDMA (Time Division Multiple Access), where time is divided into frames composed of the downlink and uplink periods.

In the downlink period, the base station communicates with the terminals through Time Division Multiplexing (TDM) and transmits the updated modulation information for users via broadcast. The modulation order is defined frame by frame based on the chosen performance criterion. In the uplink period, when users receive permission to transmit, they transmit data using TDMA. One TDMA frame is divided into X time slots, where each time slot allows the transmission of n_s bits.

In a communication system, data messages are usually transmitted in packets. In this paper, one data message containing n_d bits is fragmented into Z packets, each packet with n_s bits. Only one packet is transmitted in each time slot. In addition, each user has only one time slot per frame for their transmissions. Thus, Z frames are necessary to transmit a data message, $Z = n_d/n_s$. Figure 1 illustrates the frame structure and the transmission process in the uplink.

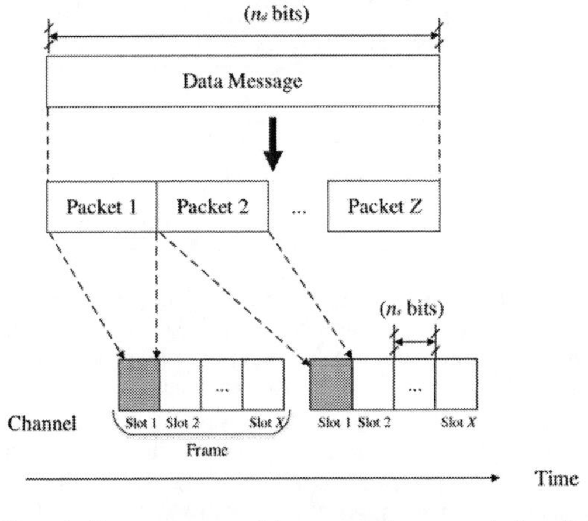

Figure 1. Frame structure and the transmission process in the uplink.

B. Channel Model

We assume a slowly-varying Nakagami-*m* block fading channel, whose complex gain values remains invariant over a single frame but may vary between adjacent frames. Thus, the choice of modulation order is made on a frame-by-frame basis [1] – [3] [6]. So, the probability density function (pdf) of the signal-to-noise ratio (SNR) is given by [2] [6]:

$$p_\gamma(\gamma) = \frac{m^m \gamma^{m-1}}{\left(\bar{\gamma}\right)^m \Gamma(m)} \exp\left(-\frac{m\gamma}{\bar{\gamma}}\right). \tag{1}$$

where $\bar{\gamma}$ is the average received SNR, $\Gamma(m)$ is the Gamma function, defined by $\Gamma(m) = \int_0^\infty x^{m-1} e^{-x} dx$, and m is the Nakagami fading parameter [2] [6].

The Nakagami-*m* probability distribution is widely used in the literature to represent a wide range of well-known multipath fades [2]. The Nakagami-*m* fading model is equivalent to a set of independent Rayleigh fading channels obtained by maximum ratio combining (MRC), where m represents the diversity order [7]. So, other distributions can be modeled with the variation of parameter m. For instance, when $m = 0.5$, the Nakagami-*m* fading model represents the unilateral Gaussian distribution (which corresponds to the greatest amount of multipath fading scenarios); when $m = 1$, the Nakagami-*m* distribution results in a Rayleigh distribution model, and when $m > 1$, there is a one-to-one mapping between the Nakagami fading parameter and the Rician factor, which allows the Nakagami distribution to approach the Rice distribution [2]. Moreover, reference [2] claims that the Nakagami-*m* distribution often provides the best fit for urban and indoor multipath propagation. Thus, in this paper, we analyze the influence of the variation of the diversity order m in the optimum switching points in an adaptive modulation scheme.

III. Calculation of the Exact PER

To compute the throughput and the delay in the network, it is necessary to compute the PER. In this section, we summarize the approach used to compute the instantaneous and average PER.

A. Instantaneous PER

In the scenario considered in this paper, the base station defines the best modulation in terms of the throughput or delay that the terminal should use to transmit data in the uplink frame. Six modulation schemes were chosen for our analysis: *M*-QAM with $M = 8, 16, 32, 64, 128$ and 256. Each *M*-ary modulation scheme has R_n bits per symbol, where $n = 1, 2\ldots 6$ and represents the modulation mode set at the moment.

In the current literature, the calculation of the PER is usually given as a function of the BER, and it is given as [6]:

$$PER = 1 - \left(1 - BER\right)^{n_s}, \tag{2}$$

where n_s represents the number of bit in a packet.

The expression (2) considers a system where the bits inside a packet have the same BER, with uncorrelated bit-errors. However, for large-size QAM constellations, the author of [6] claims that the PER calculation using (2) is not accurate since the information bits of the same packet occur with different error probabilities for such constellations.

Thus, in this paper, we considered the approach proposed by [6] to compute the PER, which is based on the methodology proposed in [8] to compute the exact BER for an arbitrary rectangular M-QAM modulation.

Following [8], we assume that a rectangular M-QAM modulation can be modeled as two independent I-ary and J-ary pulse amplitude modulations (PAM), where $M = I \times J$. The exact BER calculation is obtained by observing regular patterns that occur due to the characteristics of Gray code bit mapping. The error probability of the k_{th} bit in-phase components of the I-ary PAM , where $k \in \{1, 2, \ldots, \log_2 I\}$, is given by [8]:

$$P_I(k)=\frac{1}{I}\sum_{i=0}^{(1-2^{-k})I-1}\left\{(-1)^{\left\lfloor\frac{i\cdot 2^{k-1}}{I}\right\rfloor}\left[2^{k-1}-\left\lfloor\frac{i\cdot 2^{k-1}}{I}+\frac{1}{2}\right\rfloor\right]\right. \times\operatorname{erfc}\left.\left((2i+1)\sqrt{\frac{3\log_2(I\cdot J)\cdot\gamma_b}{I^2+J^2-2}}\right)\right\} \quad (3)$$

where $\gamma_b = E_b/N_0$ and denotes the average bit energy to noise density ratio and $\lfloor x \rfloor$ denotes the largest integer to x.

For the quadrature components of the J-ary PAM, the error probability of the l_{th} bit, where $l \in \{1, 2, \ldots, \log_2 J\}$, is obtained from [8]:

$$P_J(l)=\frac{1}{J}\sum_{j=0}^{(1-2^{-l})J-1}\left\{(-1)^{\left\lfloor\frac{j\cdot 2^{l-1}}{J}\right\rfloor}\left[2^{l-1}-\left\lfloor\frac{j\cdot 2^{l-1}}{J}+\frac{1}{2}\right\rfloor\right]\right. \times\operatorname{erfc}\left.\left((2j+1)\sqrt{\frac{3\log_2(I\cdot J)\cdot\gamma_b}{I^2+J^2-2}}\right)\right\}. \quad (4)$$

With the results obtained by (3) and (4), the authors of [6] derive an exact closed-form to compute PER. So, the exact instantaneous PER for each modulation mode in a system with rectangular QAM symbols is calculated by [6]:

$$PER_n(\gamma)=1-\left\{\prod_{k=1}^{\log_2 I}[1-P_I(k)]^{(n_s/\log_2(I\cdot J))} \times\prod_{l=1}^{\log_2 J}[1-P_J(l)]^{(n_s/\log_2(I\cdot J))}\right\}. \quad (5)$$

To compute $P_I(k)$ and $P_J(l)$, we considered $I = J = \sqrt{M}$ for square QAM modulations (256, 64 and 16-QAM), $I = 8$ and $J = 16$ for 128-QAM, $I = 4$ and $J = 8$ for 32-QAM, and finally $I = 2$ and $J = 4$ for 8-QAM.

B. Average PER

In order to consider the influence of the channel fading in the system, we initially need to find the average PER value. For each modulation, the average PER can be determined by the integral of the instantaneous PER for the current modulation (n) multiplied by the probability density function of the average symbol energy-to-noise density ratio (E_s/N_0), which in this case is the pdf of a Nakagami-m distribution [6] [9] [10]. So, the average PER is defined by:

$$\overline{PER_n}(\bar{\gamma})=\int_0^\infty PER_n(\gamma)p_\gamma(\gamma)d\gamma. \quad (6)$$

Figure 2 shows the average PER as a function of the average symbol energy-to-noise density ratio for $m = 1$, representing a channel with Rayleigh fading.

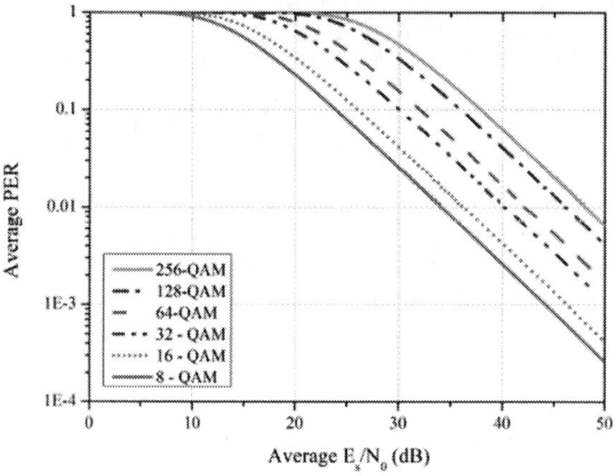

Figure 2. Average PER for a Rayleigh fading channel.

IV. The Maximum Throughput Criterion

The maximum throughput criterion has been considered in the real-time traffic scenario, where no error correction protocol was implemented. To compute the throughput, only successfully transmitted packets were considered (a parameter referred as *goodput* by some authors). We also assume an adaptive modulation scheme without error control coding, where all transmitted bits are information bits. Following [4], to compute the normalized throughput of the current modulations, we consider the following parameters:

- The ratio between the maximum number of transmitted bits and the maximum number of possible bits. In other words, the number of bits per symbol of the current modulation over the number of bits per symbol of a reference modulation;
- The percentage of packets correctly received.

So, the normalized throughput of the current modulation is given by:

$$\eta = \frac{\log_2 M_n}{\log_2 M_r} \cdot P_{cn} \tag{7}$$

where M_n is the number of points in the constellation of the current modulation, M_r is the number of points in the constellation of the reference modulation (in our case, 256-QAM) and P_{cn} is the probability of a data packet being successfully transmitted, given by:

$$P_{cn} = (1 - \overline{PER_n}(\bar{\gamma})). \tag{8}$$

In the numerical results, presented in Section VI, to compute P_{cn}, following [4], we considered that each packet has $n_s = 424$ bits.

V. Delay Criterion

In communication systems with non-real-time applications, in general, errors are corrected by retransmission using some retransmission protocol. In this context, the average time to transmit a correct data message is an important criterion to analyze the system performance [4] [5].

In our analysis, we consider that the ARQ (Automatic Repeat ReQuest) protocol is implemented at the data message level. Thus, if a single data packet is not successfully received, the entire data message is retransmitted. In this scenario, the average time to transmit a correct data message for a given modulation is given by [4]:

$$E(T)_n = \frac{T}{P_{dn}} + KT_Q \frac{(1-P_{dn})}{P_{dn}} \tag{9}$$

where T is the time required to transmit a data message disregarding channel errors, K is the mean number of frames between the end of an incorrect transmission and the start of a retransmission of a data message, T_Q is the frame time, and P_{dn} is the probability of receiving a correct data message, given by:

$$P_{dn} = \left(1 - \overline{PER_n}\left(\bar{\gamma}\right)\right)^Z \tag{10}$$

The time to transmit a data message is given by [4]:

$$T = \frac{n_s[(\mathrm{Z}-1)\mathrm{X}+1]}{\beta_n B} \tag{11}$$

where X is the number of time slots in a frame, β_n is the bandwidth efficiency of the current modulation, given by $\beta_n = \log_2 M_n$ [bps/Hz], and B is the bandwidth of the channel.

The frame time is calculated by [4]:

$$T_Q = \frac{n_s \mathrm{X}}{\beta_n B} \tag{12}$$

The optimum switching points between neighboring modulations can be determined through a performance factor (δ), defined in [4] [5] by the ratio between the average time to transmit a data message for a 2^n-QAM modulation and the average time to transmit a data message for a 2^{n-1}-QAM modulation, with n = 8, 7, 6, 5 and 4. Thus, using (9), (11) and (12), the performance factor is given by [4] [5]:

$$\delta = \frac{(Z-1)\cdot X + 1 + KX(1-P_{d(n-1)})}{(Z-1)\cdot X + 1 + KX(1-P_{dn})} \cdot \frac{\beta_n}{\beta_{n-1}} \cdot \left(\frac{P_{dn}}{P_{d(n-1)}}\right). \tag{13}$$

where $\beta_{n,\ (n-1)}$ is the bandwidth efficiency of the modulations n and $n - 1$, respectively, and $P_{dn,\ (n-1)}$ is the probability of a data message being correctly received for modulations n and $n - 1$, respectively.

VI. Numerical Results

In this section, we present numerical results for the optimum switching points using the maximum throughput criterion and delay criterion. We analyze the influence of the fading on the optimum switching points by varying the diversity order m of the Nakagami fading considering m = 0.5, 1, 2, 3 and 10, where the last value was used in order to consider an AWGN-like channel.

The calculation of the average PER is made by (3), (4), (5) and (6). Then, the PER is replaced in (8) to compute the probability that a packet was correctly received for throughput criterion and replaced in (10) to compute the probability that a data message was correctly received for delay criterion. All computations were performed using the Mathcad software.

When the system switches from one modulation to another one, the transmission power, or the average symbol energy, is kept constant. Thus, following [1] [4] [5], we analyze the system performance as a function of the parameter E_s/N_0, which represents the average symbol energy-to-noise density ratio.

A. Throughput Criterion

To calculate the normalized throughput (η), we replaced the result found by (8) in (7). We considered 256-QAM as the reference modulation and set the packet length, following [4], as $n_s = 424$ bits.

The optimum switching point between two neighboring modulations is obtained by the crossover point of the corresponding curves of the throughput (η).

Figures 3, 5, 7, 9 and 11 show the throughput curves as a function of the average symbol energy-to-noise density ratio, for 256-, 128- and 64-QAM modulations, considering m =

0.5, 1, 2, 3 and 10, respectively. Figures 4, 6, 8, 10 and 12 show the throughput curves as a function of the average symbol energy-to-noise density ratio, for 64-, 32-, 16- and 8-QAM modulations, again considering $m = 0.5$, 1, 2, 3 and 10, respectively.

Table I presents the optimum switching points and the throughput at these points. We can observe that the throughput at the switching points increases as m grows. In other words, if the channel fading becomes less severe, the throughput at these switching points increases.

In addition, we can see that the optimum points vary with the fading order (represented by the parameter m of the Nakagami model), and for a particular value of m, we can observe that the average symbol energy-to-noise density ratio in the switching points is not fixed, but varies with the neighboring modulations.

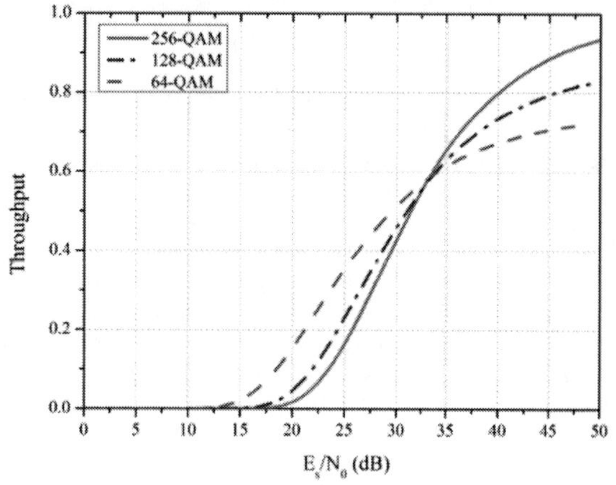

Figure 3. Throughput for $m = 0.5$ and 256, 128, and 64-QAM.

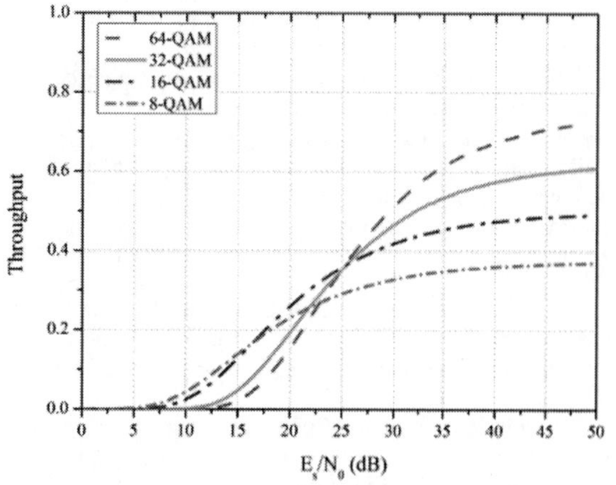

Figure 4. Throughput for $m = 0.5$ and 64, 32, 16 and 8-QAM.

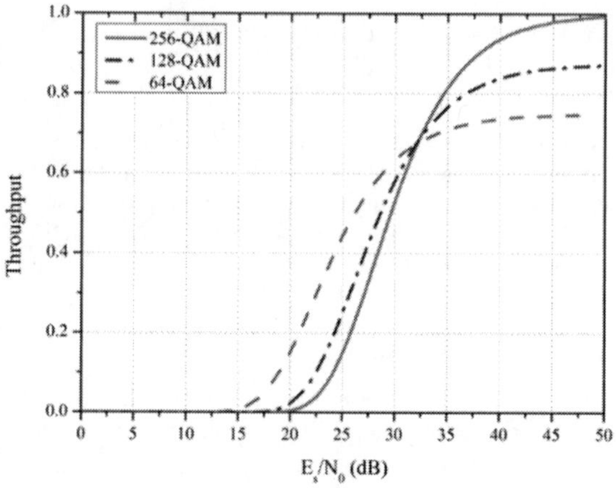

Figure 5. Throughput for $m = 1$ and 256, 128 and 64-QAM.

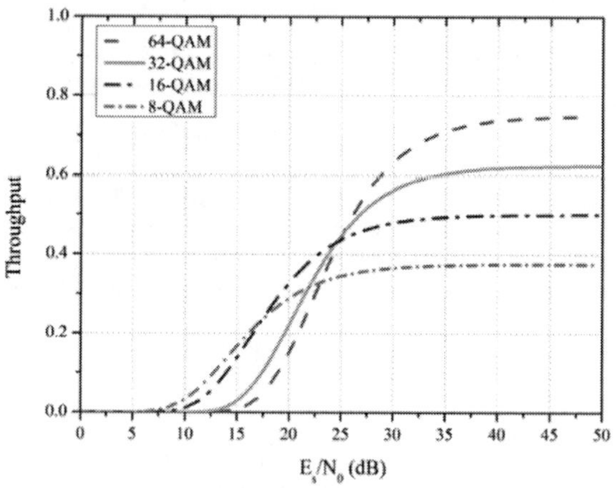

Figure 6. Throughput for $m = 1$ and 64, 32, 16 and 8-QAM.

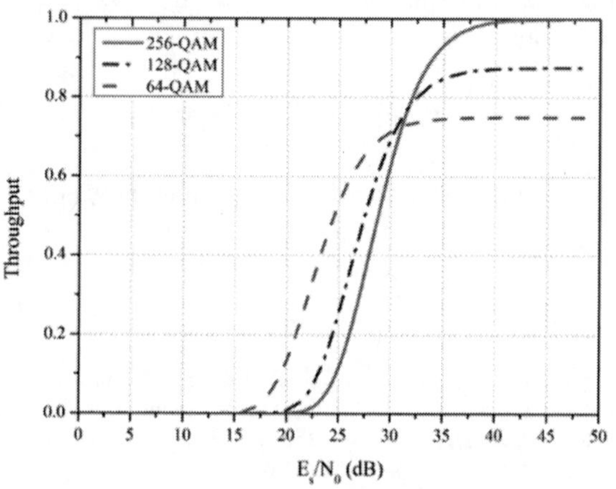

Figure 7. Throughput for $m = 2$ and 256, 128 and 64-QAM

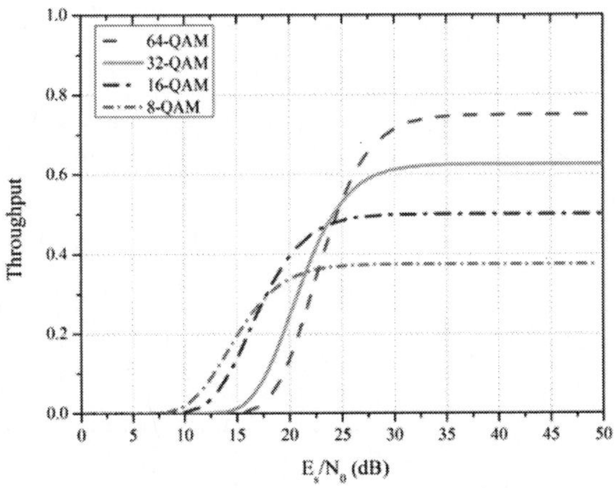

Figure 8. Throughput for $m = 2$ and 64, 32, 16 and 8-QAM.

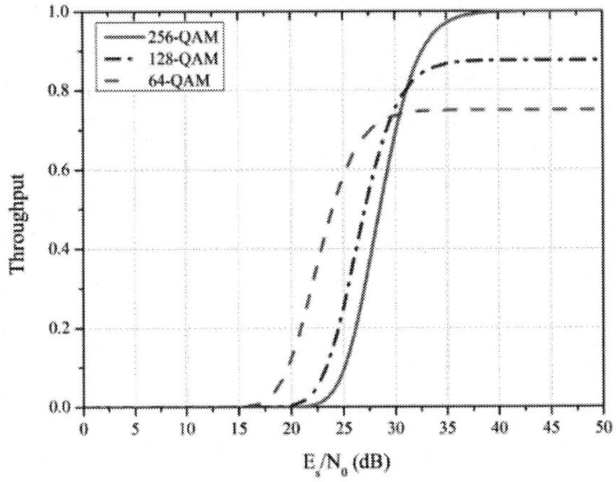

Figure 9. Throughput for $m = 3$ and 256, 128 and 64-QAM

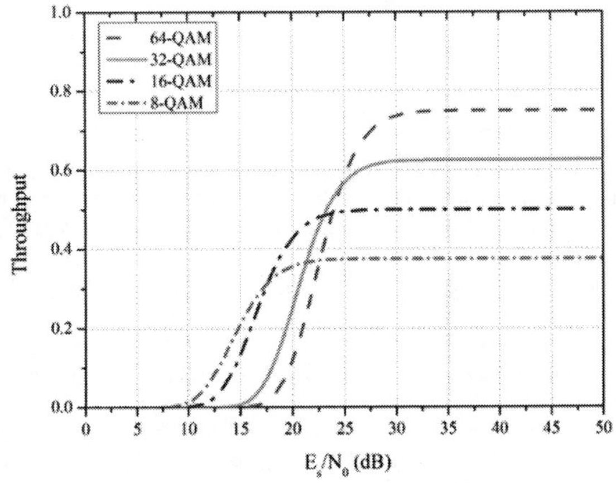

Figure 10. Throughput for $m = 3$ and 64, 32, 16 and 8-QAM

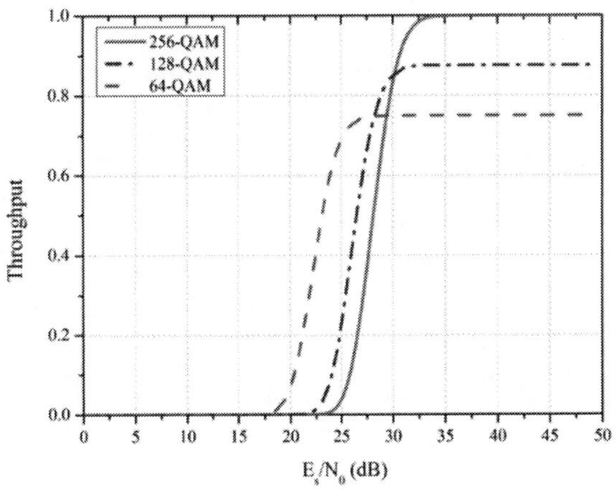

Figure 11. Throughput for $m = 10$ and 256, 128 and 64-QAM

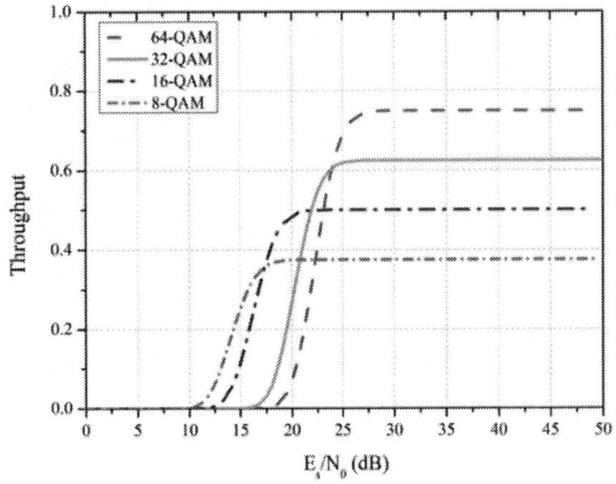

Figure 12. Throughput for $m = 10$ and 64, 32, 16 and 8-QAM.

Finally, through the analysis of Figures 3 to 12 and Table I, we can observe that some switching points between some neighboring modulations are close to each other. For example, the switching point between the neighboring modulations 256-QAM to 128-QAM is close to the switching point between the neighboring modulations 128-QAM to 64-QAM when m assumes the values $m = 1, 2, 3$ and 10. The same behavior can be observed for the switching point between the neighboring modulations 64-QAM to 32-QAM and the switching point between the neighboring modulations 32-QAM to 16-QAM. Consequently, their throughput values are also very close to each other. Therefore, we can conclude that some modulations (like 128-QAM and 32-QAM) should not be considered for the implementation of an adaptive modulation scheme when the throughput criterion is considered.

Moreover, for the case of more severe fading, when $m = 0.5$, the switching point from 128 to 64-QAM occurs before the switching point from 256 to 128-QAM. The same occurs for the switching point from 32 to 16-QAM, which occurs before the switching point from 64 to 32-QAM. So, we can conclude that 128-QAM and 32-QAM modulations should not be used in the adaptive modulation system in this case.

TABLE I. OPTIMUM SWITCHING POINTS AND NORMALIZED THROUGHPUT

Switch from	m	Switching points E_s/N_0 (dB)	Throughput (η)
256 to128-QAM	0.5	32.7	0.559
	1	32.3	0.685
	2	31.6	0.77
	3	31.2	0.806
	10	30.1	0.846
128 to 64-QAM	0.5	33.7	0.592
	1	31.9	0.671
	2	30.4	0.718
	3	29.6	0.729
	10	28.2	0.746
64 to 32-QAM	0.5	25.1	0.353
	1	25.1	0.449
	2	24.9	0.527
	3	24.6	0.553
	10	23.9	0.603
32 to 16-QAM	0.5	25.4	0.364
	1	24.5	0.429
	2	23.5	0.469
	3	23	0.484
	10	21.8	0.492
16 to 8-QAM	0.5	16.5	0.168
	1	17.3	0.231
	2	17.6	0.289
	3	17.6	0.311
	10	17.3	0.353

B. *Delay Criterion*

To compute the performance factor (δ), we employ the result obtained by (10) in (13) and, following [4], set the parameters X = 10 and K = 1. Now, the optimum switching point between two neighboring modulations is obtained by the crossover point of the curves of the performance factor (δ) with the line $\delta = 1$.

1) Analysis of the Influence of the Z:

Initially, we analyzed the influence of the length of the data message in the performance factor (δ). For this, we vary the parameter Z for a fixed slot size equal to n_s = 424 bits. Figures 13 and 14 represent the performance factor curves between modulations 256- and 128-QAM and between modulations 128- and 64-QAM, respectively, considering Z = 1, 10, 100 and 1000 and the diversity order m = 10 (approaching an AWGN channel performance). We can observe that the optimum switching point depends on the data message length. As Z increases, so will the value of E_s/N_0 at this optimum switching point.

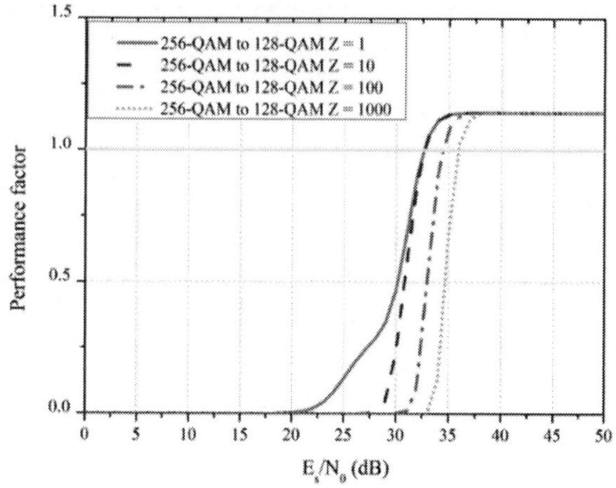

Figure 13. Performance Factor (δ) for Z = 1, 10, 100 and 1000, m = 10 and switching from 256- to 128-QAM.

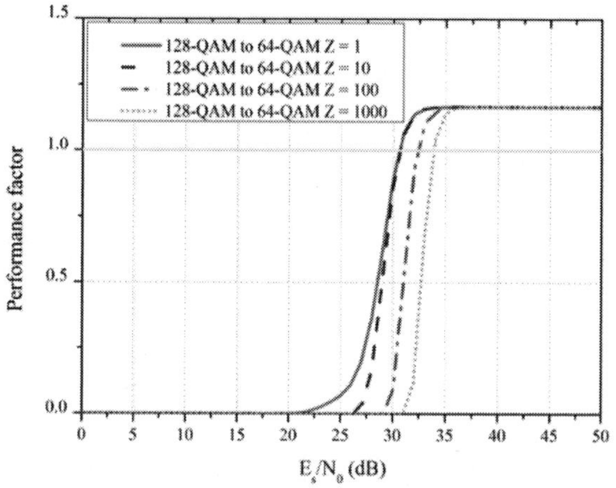

Figure 14. Performance Factor (δ) for Z = 1, 10, 100 and 1000, m = 10 and switching from 128- to 64-QAM.

2) *Comparing the results for throughput and delay criteria:*

In this section, we compare the results obtained by the maximum throughput and the delay criteria. To be fair, we set Z = 1, and we compute the optimum switching points for both criteria. As Z = 1, the number of bits in a time slot, n_s, is equal to the length of a data message, n_d. Two packet lengths are considered in our analysis: n_s = 424 and 4240 bits. Again, in order to consider the effect of the channel model in the optimum switching points, we consider the diversity order, m, equal to 0.5, 1, 2, 3 and 10.

Figures 15, 16, 17, 18 and 19 show the performance factor curves for n_s = 424 bits and m = 0.5, 1, 2, 3 and 10, respectively. Figures 20, 21, 22, 23 and 24 show the performance factor curves for m = 0.5, 1, 2, 3 and 10, respectively, but consider a larger packet size, $n_s = 4240$ bits. The performance factor curves in these figures are between the following modulations: 256- and 128-QAM, 128- and 64-QAM, 64- and 32-QAM, 32- and 16-QAM, and 16- and 8-QAM.

Table II shows the optimum switching points between neighboring modulations for $n_s = 424$ bits for both criteria. Table III shows the same but now considering $n_s = 4240$ bits.

TABLE II. THE OPTIMUM SWITCHING POINTS FOR THROUGHPUT AND DELAY CRITERION $n_s = 424$ bits

Switch from	m	Switching points E_s/N_0 (dB) for throughput criterion	Switching points E_s/N_0 (dB) for delay criterion
256 to128-QAM	0.5	32.7	45.4
	1	32.3	41.5
	2	31.6	37.4
	3	31.2	35.6
	10	30.1	32.5
128 to 64-QAM	0.5	33.7	49.6
	1	31.9	41.6
	2	30.4	36.1
	3	29.6	34
	10	28.2	30.5
64 to 32-QAM	0.5	25.1	34.9
	1	25.1	33.7
	2	24.9	30.7
	3	24.6	29.1
	10	23.9	26.4
32 to 16-QAM	0.5	25.4	39.4
	1	24.5	33.9
	2	23.5	29.3
	3	23	27.4
	10	21.8	24.3
16 to 8-QAM	0.5	16.5	22.6
	1	17.3	24.8
	2	17.6	23.3
	3	17.6	22.2
	10	17.3	19.8

Analyzing Tables II and III, and the Figures 15 to 24, we can observe that the optimum switching points for the delay criterion assume values of Es/N_0 larger than the optimum switching points for the throughput criterion. Thus, the optimum switching points depend on of the considered criterion. We can also see that the greater the length of the data message, the larger is the Es/N_0 in the optimum switching points.

We can observe again that the optimum switching points change as m varies. Thus, the optimum switching points depend on the channel model.

TABLE III. THE OPTIMUM SWITCHING POINTS FOR THROUGHPUT AND DELAY CRITERION $n_s = 4240$ bits

Switch from	m	Switching points E_s/N_0 (dB) for throughput criterion	Switching points E_s/N_0 (dB) for delay criterion
256 to128-QAM	0.5	34.8	47.5
	1	34.3	43.5
	2	33.6	39.3
	3	33.1	37.4
	10	31.9	34
128 to 64-QAM	0.5	35.7	51.6
	1	33.9	43.5
	2	32.2	37.9
	3	31.5	35.7
	10	29.9	32
64 to 32-QAM	0.5	27	37.1
	1	27.1	35.7
	2	26.8	32.5
	3	26.5	30.9
	10	25.6	27.9
32 to 16-QAM	0.5	27.3	41.4
	1	26.4	35.7
	2	25.3	31
	3	24.8	29
	10	23.5	25.7
16 to 8-QAM	0.5	18.4	24.6
	1	19.2	26.7
	2	19.5	25.1
	3	19.5	23.9
	10	19.1	21.3

It can also be seen that the average symbol energy-to-noise density in the optimum switching points using the delay criterion decreases as m increases.

Similarly to the throughput criterion, in the case of the delay criterion and $m = 0.5$, the switching point from 128- to 64-QAM occurs before the switching point from 256- to 128-QAM for both values of n_s. In addition, the switching point from 32- to 16-QAM occurs before the switching point from 64- to 32-QAM. Thus, again, for $m = 0.5$, the modulations 128-QAM and 32-QAM should not be used in the adaptive modulation system if the delay criterion is used.

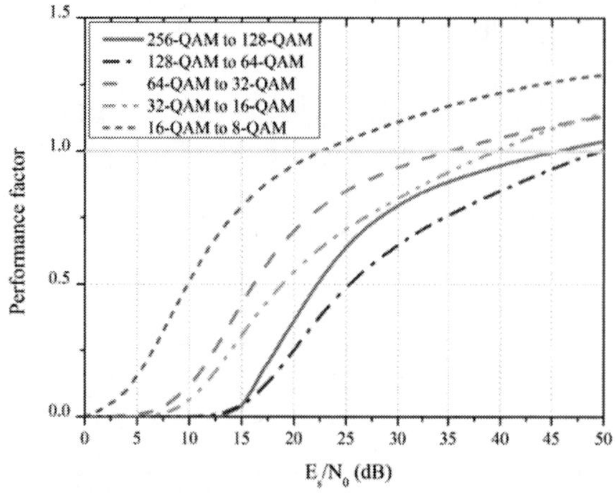

Figure 15. Performance Factor (δ) for Z = 1, n_s = 424, m = 0.5, and (256,128), (128,64), (64,32), (32,16) and (16,8) QAM pairs.

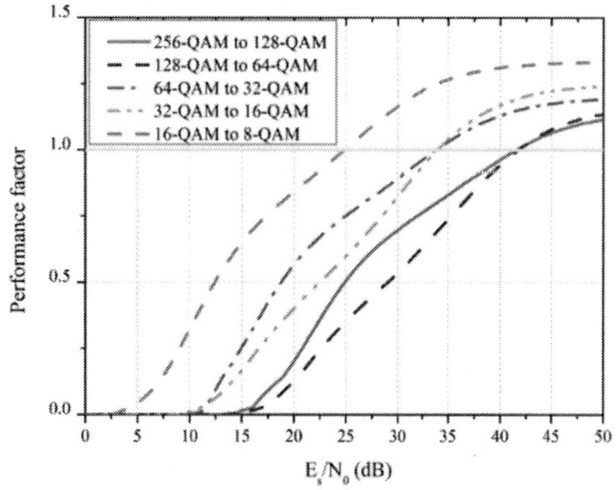

Figure 16. Performance Factor (δ) for Z = 1, n_s = 424, m = 1, and (256,128), (128,64), (64,32), (32,16) and (16,8) QAM pairs.

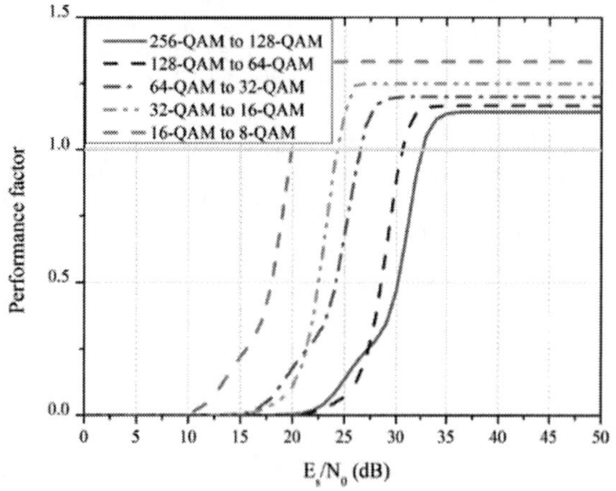

Figure 17. Performance Factor (δ) for Z = 1, n_s = 424, m = 2, and (256,128), (128,64), (64,32), (32,16) and (16,8) QAM pairs.

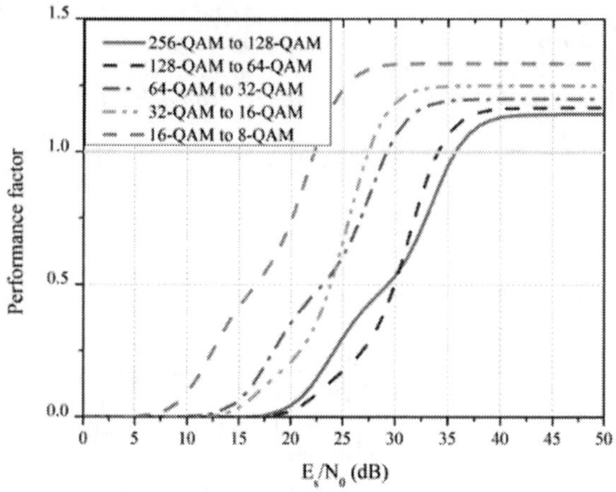

Figure 18. Performance Factor (δ) for Z = 1, n_s = 424, m = 3, and (256,128), (128,64), (64,32), (32,16) and (16,8) QAM pairs.

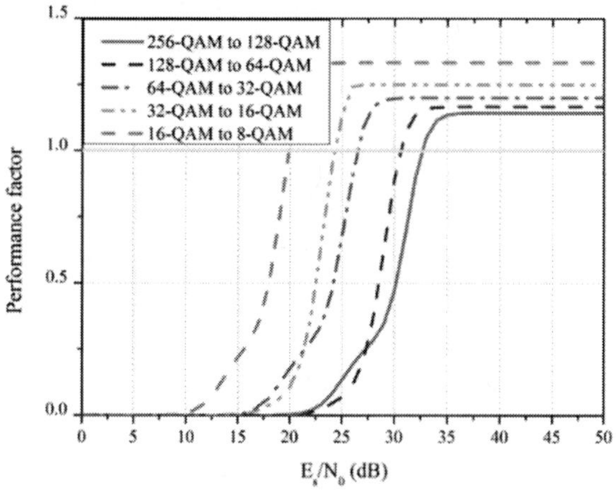

Figure 19. Performance Factor (δ) for Z = 1, n_s = 424, m = 10, and (256,128), (128,64), (64,32), (32,16) and (16,8) QAM pairs.

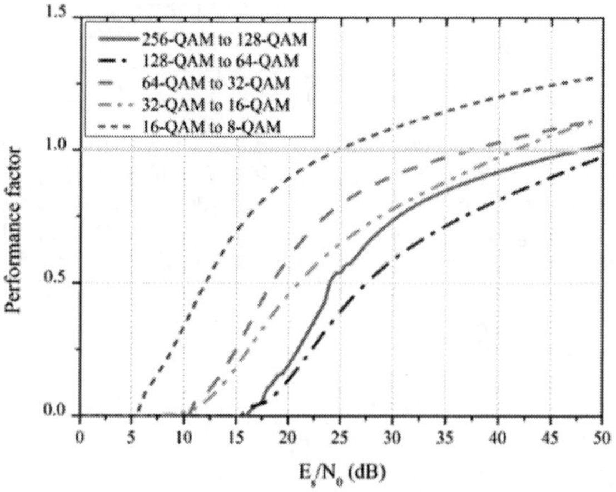

Figure 20. Performance Factor (δ) for Z = 1, n_s = 4240, m = 0.5, and (256,128), (128,64), (64,32), (32,16) and (16,8) QAM pairs.

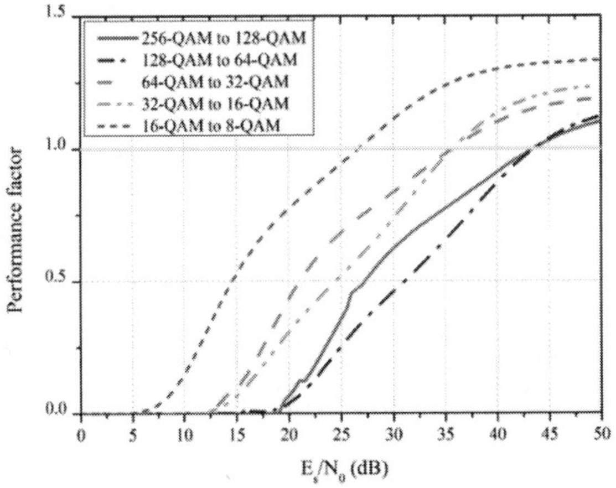

Figure 21. Performance Factor (δ) for Z = 1, n_s = 4240, m = 1, and (256,128), (128,64), (64,32), (32,16) and (16,8) QAM pairs.

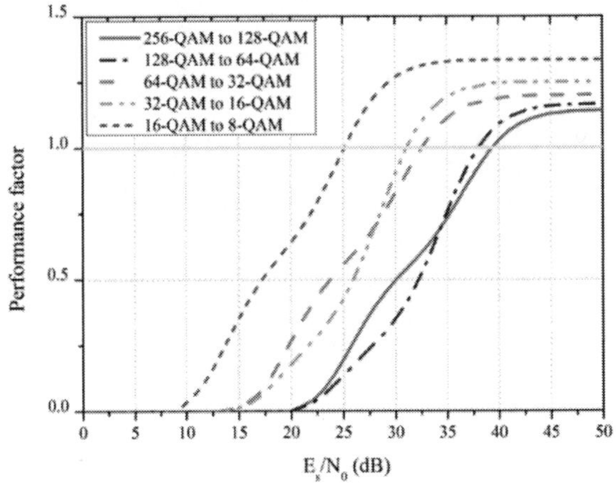

Figure 22. Performance Factor (δ) for Z = 1, n_s = 4240, m = 2, and (256,128), (128,64), (64,32), (32,16) and (16,8) QAM pairs.

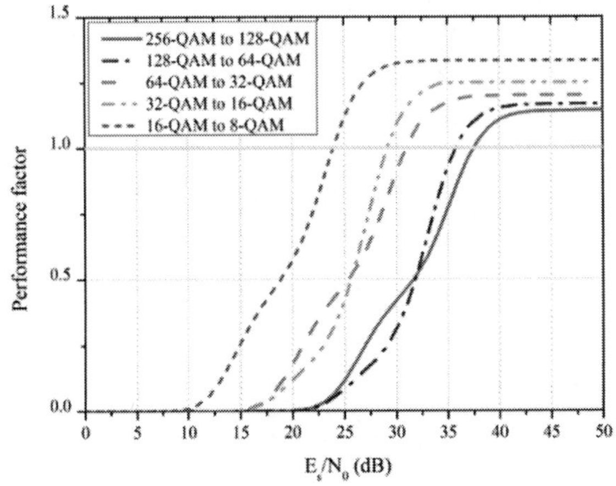

Figure 23. Performance Factor (δ) for Z = 1, n_s = 4240, m = 3, and (256,128), (128,64), (64,32), (32,16) and (16,8) QAM pairs.

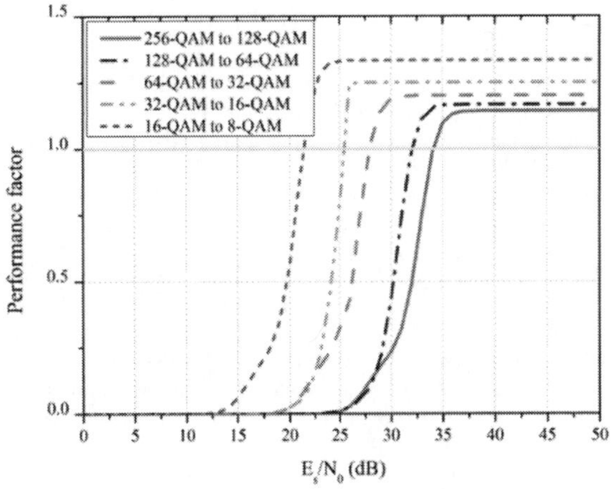

Figure 24. Performance Factor (δ) for Z = 1, n_s = 4240, m = 10, and (256,128), (128,64), (64,32), (32,16) and (16,8) QAM pairs.

VII. Conclusion

In this paper, we considered a system with adaptive modulation and a Nakagami-m fading channel. We analyzed the influence of the channel model in the optimum switching points between neighboring modulations considering two scenarios: real-time and non-real-time traffic. To compute these points, we employed the maximum throughput criterion for real-time traffic and the mean time to transmit a data message for non-real-time traffic. We considered M-QAM modulations, with M = 8, 16, 32, 64, 128 and 256, and we varied the diversity order of the channel setting, i.e., m = 0.5, 1, 2, 3 and 10.

We concluded that the optimum switching points depend on the channel model and on the type of the traffic in the system (real-time and non-real-time traffic) that defines the best criterion to compute the switching points.

We also observed that for the throughput criterion, some modulations (like 128-QAM and 32-QAM) can be neglected in the implementation of a practical adaptive modulation scheme.

Furthermore, for systems where the fading channel is severe (m = 0.5), the switching point from 128- to 64-QAM occurs before the switching point from 256- to 128-QAM, and the switching point from 32- to 16-QAM occurs before the switching point from 64- to 32-QAM, for both criteria (throughput and delay). Therefore, 128-QAM and 32-QAM should not be used in the adaptive modulation system in this case.

Acknowledgment

This work was partially supported by Finep, with resources from Funttel, Grant No. 01.14.0231.00, under the Radiocommunication Reference Center (Centro de Referência em Radiocomunicações - CRR) project of the National Institute of Telecommunications (Instituto Nacional de Telecomunicações - Inatel), Brazil.

REFERENCES

[1] A. P. T. R. da Silva and J. M. C. Brito, "Influence of the Channel Model in the Optimum Switching Points in an Adaptive Modulation System," in Proc. ICN 2016, The Fifteenth International Conference on Networks, pp. 7–12, Feb. 2016.

[2] M.-S. Alouini and A. J. Goldsmith, "Adaptive Modulation over Nakagami Fading Channels," Wirel. Pers. Commun., vol. 13, no. 1–2, pp. 119–143, May 2000.

[3] T. Quazi and H. Xu, "Performance analysis of adaptive M-QAM over a flat-fading Nakagami-m channel," South Afr. J. Sci., vol. 107, no. 1–2, pp. 1–7, Feb. 2011.

[4] J. M. C. Brito and I. S. Bonatti, "Analysing the optimal threshold level for adaptive modulation in the wireless ATM networks," Proc Iasted Int. Conf. Wirel. Opt. Commun. Banf Can., pp. 510–515, Jul. 2002.

[5] M. S. Y. Bandiri and J. M. C. Brito, "Analyzing the Optimum Switching Points for Adaptive Modulation in Wireless Networks with Rayleigh Fading," 6th IEEE Lat.-Am. Conf. Commun, six pages, Nov. 2014.

[6] Q. Liu, S. Zhou, and G. B. Giannakis, "Cross-Layer combining of adaptive Modulation and coding with truncated ARQ over wireless links," IEEE Trans. Wirel. Commun., vol. 3, no. 5, pp. 1746–1755, Sep. 2004.

[7] Z. Wang and G. B. Giannakis, "A simple and general parameterization quantifying performance in fading channels," IEEE Trans. Commun., vol. 51, no. 8, pp. 1389–1398, Aug. 2003.

[8] K. Cho and D. Yoon, "On the general BER expression of one- and two-dimensional amplitude modulations," IEEE Trans. Commun., vol. 50, no. 7, pp. 1074–1080, Jul. 2002.

[9] Y. Xi, A. Burr, J. Wei, and D. Grace, "A General Upper Bound to Evaluate Packet Error Rate over Quasi-Static Fading Channels," IEEE Trans. Wirel. Commun., vol. 10, no. 5, pp. 1373–1377, May 2011.

[10] A. J. de Faria and J. M. C. Brito, "A New Throughput Analysis in Cognitive Radio Networks Using Slotted CSMA," presented at the COCORA 2013, The Third International Conference on Advances in Cognitive Radio, pp. 1–6, Apr. 2013.

Performance Analysis of Mobile IPv6 under Spectrum Mobility in Cognitive Radio (CR) Networks

Manoj Kumar Rana
SMCC
Jadavpur University
Kolkata, India
e-mail: manoj24.rana@gmail.com

Swarup Mandal
Delivery Head
Wipro Limited
Kolkata, India
e-mail: swarup.mandal@wipro.com

Bhaskar Sardar
Dept of IT
Jadavpur University
Kolkata, India
e-mail: bhaskargit@yahoo.co.in

Debashis Saha
MIS Group,
Indian Institute of Management (IIM)
Calcutta, Kolkata, India
e-mail: ds@iimcal.ac.in

Abstract— **In cognitive radio (CR) networks, the secondary users may encounter frequent IP handoffs due to high spectrum mobility, even if they remain static spatially. Since mobile IPv6 (MIPv6) is not originally designed to deal gracefully with such IP handoffs induced by spectrum mobility only, the performance of the IP-based applications running in secondary users (SUs) may degrade severely in such scenarios. This paper conducts a simulation based investigation to gauge the seriousness of the issue and then suggests possible solutions. To do so, we have first developed in ns-3 a CR Attribute Module, and then implemented MIPv6 over it. For SUs, we have considered three spectrum selection strategies, namely Greedy, Most Recently Used, and Least Frequently Used. In each case, we have analyzed how the frequency of IP handoffs varies with the rise in spectrum mobility, resulting in degraded throughput in SUs. Our study reveals that MIPv6 is unable to work properly in CR networks mainly due to the high default values of MIPv6 parameters. So, we propose to customize mobile IPv6 – in terms of appropriating the pre-set values of its parameters – in order to make it work properly in CR networks, especially where the spectrum mobility is high.**

Keywords- Cognitive Radio Network; Spectrum Mobility; Simulation; ns-3; Mobile IPv6 (MIPv6); IP handoff.

I. INTRODUCTION

The ever-increasing popularity of mobile devices and smart phones are causing explosive growth of data traffic in mobile communication networks [1]-[4]. At the same time, the *licensed* spectrum for mobile broadband is becoming limited and hence costly to the mobile operators. However, recent surveys on spectrum occupancy statistics in various countries worldwide reveal that licensed bands are not being utilized fully [3]. This opens up the possibility that a user of a heavily loaded system can harness the underutilized spectrum of another system opportunistically. The well-known approach of dynamic spectrum access employs the cognitive radio (CR) technique, which has been standardized in IEEE 1900.4 [4] and included in the end-to-end efficiency project of the European Telecommunication Standard Institute (ETSI) [5]. According to IEEE 1900.4 [4] and ITU-R M.2330-0 report [6], opportunistic spectrum usage could be another deployment scenario of CR-based dynamic spectrum access in heterogeneous CR networks (CRNs). In CRNs, the base stations/access points (BSs/APs) are assumed to be legacy, operating in a particular radio access technology (RAT), whereas mobile devices, called secondary users (SUs), are reconfigurable terminals (can use different frequency bands of radio access networks (RANs)). Utilization of idle licensed spectrum in this way reduces the capital expenditure as no extra investment is needed for new system installations.

An SU in a CRN switches from one channel to another, when it is interrupted by a licensed device, commonly known as primary user (PU). This event of channel switching is called *spectrum mobility* [7]. Spectrum mobility in a multi-RAT, multi RAN and multi-operator environment causes two types of handoff: *intra-system* handoff and *inter-system* handoff [4]. Switching from a busy channel to a free channel of the same network system at the time of PU arrival causes an intra-system handoff. On the contrary, switching from a busy channel of one network system to a free channel of a different network system at the time of PU arrival is called an inter-system handoff. Inter-system handoff happens typically in a heterogeneous radio environment, where multiple operators use multi-RATs in the same location (for example, Fig. 1). In Fig. 1, one operator has WCDMA commercial network (i.e., a cellular system), while another operator owns IEEE 802.11x technology as a private WLAN system. In such a muti-RAT, multi-operator scenario, inter-system handoff is a major challenge because the conventional handoff management schemes (such as GPRS tunneling protocol used in 3G systems, or, the complex tunneling mechanism, used in Long Term Evolution (LTE)) used to perform handoff between the same RAT within the same operator's network. Hence, they can be solely based on link layer technology. As a result, these techniques are not suitable for heterogeneous CRNs.

So, there is a strong need to migrate the technology-specific core infrastructure toward all-IP platform, since IP is generic enough to serve all underlying technologies. Although there are numerous IP-based handoff management protocols, we consider mobile IPv6 (MIPv6) [9] in this work because it is the de-facto standard in today's world. As reported by ITU-R [6], the inter-system handoff can be handled through IP layer by implementing a dedicated radio system as the common signaling channel, called basic access network (BAN) [8]. It employs a cognitive pilot channel, standardized in the E3 project, to inform the SUs about the access information, such as the available channels, relevant load and access strategy of each RAT. Due to the dynamic behaviour of radio networks, BANs adopt a handoff strategy that uses the environmental radio information (i.e., channel idleness), useful for opportunistic SUs to switch to the preferred network. The cognitive pilot channel consumes small bandwidth of a licensed/unlicensed channel as reported in [6]. It is used for the sole purpose of signaling only, and not for data transmission.

The focus of our work in this paper is on the performance evaluation of inter-system handoffs caused by spectrum mobility only [10]. We assume that the unavailability of channels in the current network causes an inter-system handoff that ultimately leads to an IP handoff. Thus, eventually, the frequency of IP handoffs depends on the parameters, such as PU arrival rate and PU channel holding time [11]. In CRNs, the number of such IP handoffs may be quite high even when the SU is stationary (i.e., mobility-driven handoffs are practically zero). Moreover, in modern WLAN and LTE or LTE-Advanced (LTE-A) networks, the channel usage occurs in discontinuous mode, i.e., a PU uses a channel for its transmission for a short duration, and then immediately releases the channel for the other PUs [12]. For instance, on an average if a PU has 2^{10} bytes of data to transmit and its transmission rate is 20 Kbps, its average channel holding time is 0.4 s (=(2^{10}*8)/20000). Also, 80% of the spectrum holes in a WLAN are not very big, being only 0-3 s wide [13]. Given such small channel holding times as well as narrow spectrum holes, PU interruption frequency becomes very high. It renders the CRN environment extremely dynamic for the SUs. This, in turn, poses a new set of challenges for the MIPv6 [9] itself because even if the SUs are static, they have to invoke MIPv6 to handle IP handoffs triggered by spectrum mobility.

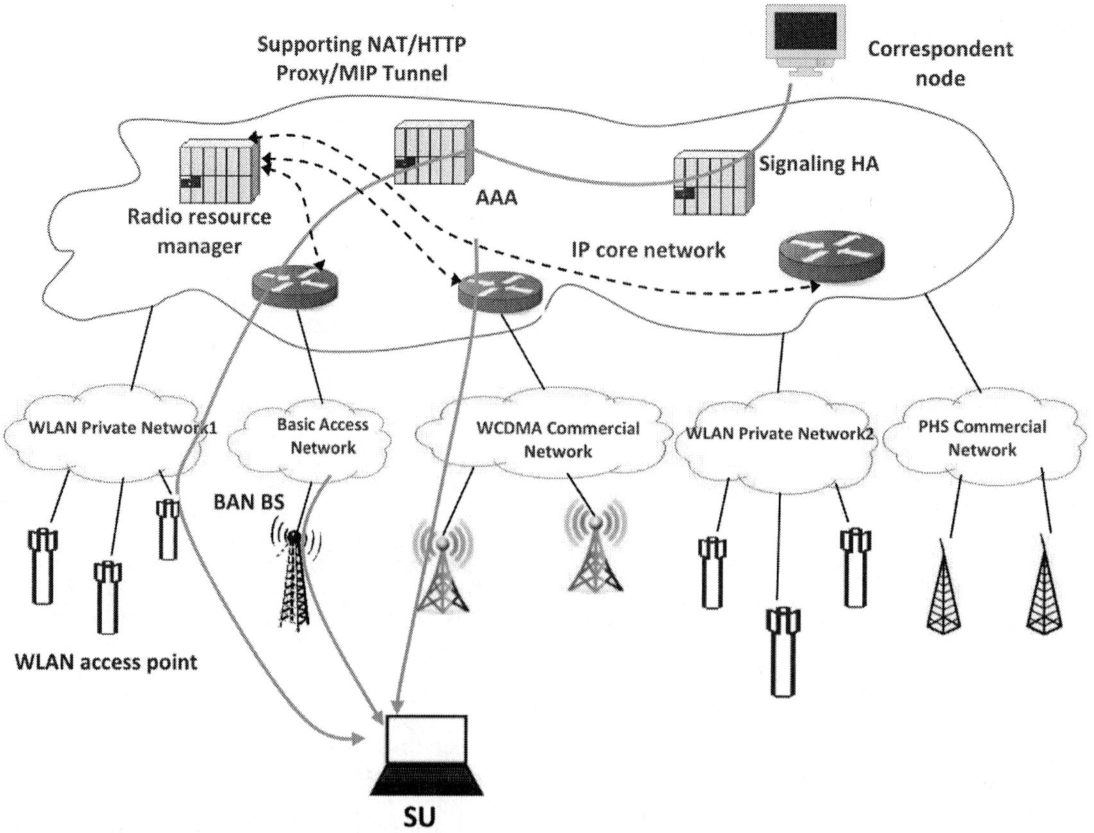

Figure 1. Heterogeneous CR networks: cross-operator handoff with MIP support

MIPv6 was originally designed for handling spatial mobility only, and so it is not optimized for frequent IP handoffs due to inter-system spectrum mobility. It is well known that the handoff procedure in MIPv6 takes a significant amount of time, approximately 1.896 s to 2.47 s [14]. Hence, the net temporal overhead due to multiple IP handoffs may become very high over the complete lifetime of a data connection for an SU, which degrades its data throughput significantly. That is why the objective of this paper is to investigate the performance of MIPv6 in CRNs, in particular, the effect of spectrum mobility on MIPv6. We know that, depending on the movement detection and care-of-address (CoA) configuration strategies, the standard MIPv6 has three flavors: router advertisement (RA) based MIPv6 [9], router solicitation (RS) based MIPv6 [9] and dynamic host configuration protocol (DHCP) based MIPv6 [9][15]. In the first two flavors, an SU uses a stateless address auto-configuration mechanism to configure new CoA. In the third flavor, the DHCP server assigns IP addresses through a dynamic address allocation method [15]. We have performed our analyses using all the three flavors of MIPv6. To simulate a heterogeneous CRN, we have developed the following modules in the network simulator ns-3 [16]: (1) a CR attribute module (CRAM) to mimic a typical CRN, (2) three basic spectrum selection algorithms, namely greedy (GDY), most recently used (MRU), and least frequently used (LFU), and (3) our own MIPv6 module [17] as per RFC 6275 [9].

Our main purpose is to identify exact causes behind the afore-mentioned issues of MIPv6 (in all the three flavors) when used in CRNs. We have investigated the simulation traces and observed that the high values of RA interval, lifetime of CoA, and duplicate address detection (DAD) timers are primarily responsible for the poor performance of MIPv6. Next, we have validated the numerical results with our simulation results. Finally, we have suggested the suitable values for CoA lifetime and DAD period for possible use in heterogeneous CRNs. Also, we have measured the throughput performance of SUs for different spectrum selection algorithms, by varying the PU arrival rate and PU channel holding time. It is worth mentioning here that this paper is an extended version of [1] to report additional numerical analyses, wide-ranging simulation results, new validation exercises, and explanatory notes.

The rest of the paper is organized as follows. In Section II, we discuss recent research works on spectrum handoff and IP handoff in CRNs. Section III provides a brief description of our model implementations in ns-3. Section IV illustrates the MIPv6 issues noted in the considered heterogeneous CRNs. In Section V, we have analyzed the number of IP handoffs and its impact on throughput of the SUs. Finally, Section VI recommends the suitable modifications needed to overcome the issues with MIPv6.

II. Related Works

To access the Internet services using CRNs, the SUs cycle through three sequential phases: *spectrum handoff* phase, *IP handoff* phase, and *data transmission* phase. The spectrum handoff phase consists of channel sensing, handoff decision, pause, and channel switching functions [7]. Similarly, IP handoff phase consists of RA, CoA formation, and tunnel setup [9]. The phase transition is illustrated in Fig. 2. During data transmission, if reappearance of PU occurs, then the SU moves again to channel sensing phase, where the SU attempts to find spectrum holes to switch to. If an empty channel is unavailable, the SU continues sensing the set of busy channels, repeating channel sensing and pause phases continuously. In the spectrum decision phase, the SU decides the best channel to switch to, among the available channels. The selection logic is closely related to the channel characteristics, and the operations of the PUs and the SUs. In the channel switch phase, the SU changes its operating channel. If the channel switch occurs in the same system, data transmission resumes immediately; otherwise, the SU encounters an additional IP handoff.

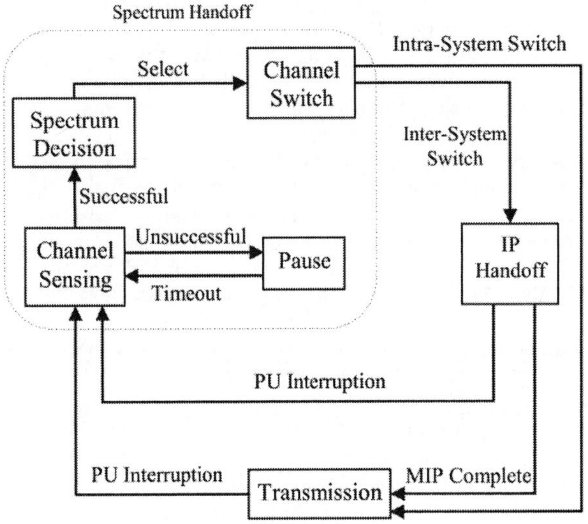

Figure 2. Mobility phase diagram in CRNs

Though many recent research works focus on spectrum mobility in CRNs, only a few of those focus on the resulting IP handoffs and problems thereof faced by SUs. Some of the previous works try to reduce MIPv6 handoff delay in heterogeneous CRNs, through integrated system architecture [10] and using a cross-layer protocol [11].

A. Spectrum Handoff

Wang et al. [18][19] have proposed a dynamic programming based greedy algorithm to determine the optimal target channel sequence, and proved that the greedy algorithm provides the same results as the dynamic programming based algorithm, but with lower time complexity. To optimize the data delivery time, a traffic-adaptive spectrum handoff mechanism is proposed in [19]. It changes the target channel sequence of spectrum handoffs based on traffic conditions. Southwell et al. [20] analyzed spectrum handoff delay, considering the cost of channel switching and congestion due to multiple SUs, with prior knowledge of heterogeneous channels. They have proposed a fast algorithm to determine the best single-user decision, depending on other user's plans without communicating with each other.

B. IP Handoff

In [10], Kataoka et al. have proposed an MIP-based CRN architecture to reduce the handoff delay. The system architecture contains a control node that integrates multi-RAT access points and a unified authentication, authorization and accounting (AAA) server that performs authentication, authorization and charging on behalf of all networks. The AAA server provides a single IP address to SUs while roaming among multiple networks and a control node manages the IP handoff through a fast routing based scheme. However, the downside of this protocol is that the control node becomes a bottleneck and this may result in a single point failure. Chen et al. [11] have proposed a cross-layer protocol to optimize the data transmission time in CR LTE networks. Since the authors have assumed homogeneous LTE networks, they have not used MIPv6. Instead they have used the standard LTE handoff mechanism which takes only a few ms; so there is not much impact of IP handoff on transmission time.

The above existing proposals have been made to reduce the IP handoff latency in CRNs. They are unable to report thus far the issues of network layer mobility management protocols, such as MIPv6 in CRNs. Also, no prior works exist to show the impact of spectrum mobility alone on MIPv6. These observations call for a detailed analysis of MIPv6 in heterogeneous CRNs, which may give us an insight into the practical design issues of MIPv6 and the impact of spectrum mobility on IP handoffs.

III. Cognitive Radio Attribute Model (CRAM)

We have implemented CRAM in ns-3 [16]. It takes traffic parameters and spectrum selection strategy as input. We describe CRAM in the following three subsections.

A. Traffic Parameters

We consider *network1* with *C1* number of channels and *network2* with *C2* number of channels. At any point in time, each of these channels can be occupied by a PU or an SU or remains empty. We have assumed that *network2* has higher preference over *network1* for SUs, i.e., an SU switches to *network1* if and only if *network2* is unavailable. For simplicity, we have assumed homogeneous traffic parameters for all channels and the PU traffic parameters are same for *network1* and *network2*. We have assumed that the PU and SU arrival processes follow a Poisson distribution while their service times follow an exponential distribution. Table I lists the variables used in this section.

Using Little's formula, we can write

$$\rho_p = \lambda_p E[X_p] \quad (1)$$

$$\rho_{s,1} = \lambda_{s,1} E[X_s] \quad (2)$$

$$\rho_{s,2} = \lambda_{s,2} E[X_s] \quad (3)$$

To calculate the arrival rate for SUs for both the networks, we use the state transition diagram shown in Fig. 3

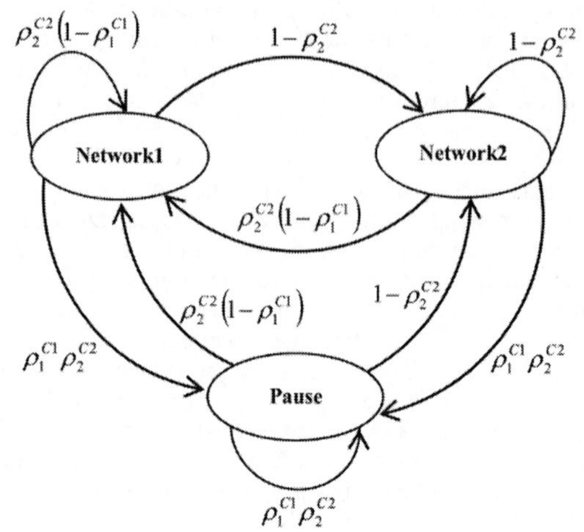

Figure 3. State transition diagram of network switching by SUs

that depicts the probabilities of network switching as a function of ρ_1 and ρ_2. The SU enters *network2* if there exists at least one empty channel and enters *network1* if all the channels of *network2* are busy and at least one empty channel is available in *network1*. So, $\lambda_{s,1}$ and $\lambda_{s,2}$ can be computed as follows:

$$\lambda_{s,1} = \left(1-\rho_1^{C1}\right)\rho_2^{C2}\lambda_s \quad (4)$$

$$\lambda_{s,2} = \left(1-\rho_2^{C2}\right)\lambda_s \quad (5)$$

TABLE I. Traffic Parameters

Parameters	Meaning
C1	Number of channels in network1
C2	Number of channels in network2
λ_p	PU arrival rate
λ_s	SU arrival rate
$\lambda_{s,1}$	SU arrival rate in network1
$\lambda_{s,2}$	SU arrival rate in network2
X_p	Service time for PUs
$E[X_p]$	Average service time for PUs
μ_p	Average expected Service rate of PUs with mean $1/E[X_p]$
μ_s	Average expected Service rate of SUs with mean $1/E[X_s]$
X_s	Service time for SUs
$E[X_s]$	Average service time for SUs
ρ_p	Channel busy probability or utilization factor by PUs
ρ_s	Channel utilization factor or channel busy probability by SUs, if it is served by network2 only
ρ_1	Overall channel utilization factors or channel busy probability by PUs in network1
ρ_2	Overall channel utilization factors or, channel busy probability by SUs in network2
$\rho_{s,1}$	Channel busy probabilities by SUs in network1
$\rho_{s,2}$	Channel busy probabilities by SUs in network2
$E[N_s]$	Average number of SUs
I_p	Inter-arrival time of the PUs
W	Spectrum hole duration

Now, $\rho_s = \lambda_s E[X_s]$, is the channel utilization factor for the SU, if it is served by *network2* only. Using the values of $\lambda_{s,1}$ and $\lambda_{s,2}$ (obtained using (4) and (5)), from (2) and (3) we get the following equations:

$$\rho_{s,1} = \left(1-\rho_1^{C1}\right)\rho_2^{C2}\rho_s \quad (6)$$

$$\rho_{s,2} = \left(1-\rho_2^{C2}\right)\rho_s \quad (7)$$

Hence, the overall channel utilization for *network1* and *network2* are calculated as:

$$\rho_1 = \rho_p + \rho_{s,1} \quad (8)$$

$$\rho_2 = \rho_p + \rho_{s,2} \quad (9)$$

To obtain ρ_s, we use M/M/C queuing model, where C denotes the number of channels being used to serve the SUs. From the definition of M/M/C queue, the average number of SUs in the system can be written as [21]:

$$E[N_S] = C\rho_s + \frac{\rho_s}{1-\rho_s} D\left(C, \frac{\lambda_s}{\mu_s}\right) \quad (10)$$

where

$$D\left(C, \frac{\lambda_S}{\mu_S}\right) = \frac{\frac{(C\rho_S)^C}{C!}\frac{1}{1-\rho_S}}{\sum_{k=0}^{C-1}\frac{(C\rho_S)^k}{k!} + \frac{(C\rho_S)^C}{C!}\frac{1}{1-\rho_S}} \quad (11)$$

which is Erlang's C formula. Using the above formula, we can compute ρ_s, taking $E[N_s]$ as input and replacing C by $C2$. Using (6), (7), (8) and (9), we can numerically solve for ρ_1 and ρ_2.

It is to be noted that the PU inter-arrival time is memory-less and follows exponential distribution with rate λ_p. The distribution of W is the difference of the distributions of I_p and X_p. So the probability mass function of W can be given as follows:

$$f(W=t) = \int_0^{\infty} P(I_p = x+t)P(X_p = x)dx = \frac{\lambda_p \mu_p}{\lambda_p + \mu_p} e^{-t\lambda_p} \quad (12)$$

B. Spectrum Selection Strategies

We have implemented three spectrum selection strategies: GDY [18][22], MRU [23], and LFU [24]. These strategies are implemented based on the statistical information of the channels. In GDY strategy, the SU selects the first empty channel without any pre-estimation of its freeness. The works in [18] and [22] on modeling and analysis of spectrum mobility events assumed GDY strategy (called first-come-first-served in their system model). The GDY strategy is an opportunistic one; it selects the first empty channel, not targeting to utilize the spectrum holes optimally [18]. In contrast, several other research works [10][23][24] adopt selection strategies to utilize spectrum holes efficiently for the purpose of load balancing among channels as well as reducing data transmission time and improving throughput of SUs. These works consider the typical heterogeneous CRN environment [10] with multiple PUs and SUs [18][23][24]. We also assume this type of scenario in this work. The MRU and LFU are selected as two efficient spectrum selection strategies based on the concepts applied in [23] and [24], respectively. In the MRU strategy, the SU selects the channel which has been used most recently by a PU, expecting a lengthy absence of PUs in that channel in the near future. In LFU strategy, the SU selects the channel which has been least used by the PUs thus far, hoping that it will remain so in the near future too. We have assumed the arrival process of PUs follow Poisson distribution. The GDY strategy selects an idle channel randomly, not considering the available spectrum hole duration. On the other hand, the LFU strategy enhances the utilization rate of a low utilized channel. But, accessing the channel which has been used by a PU most recently, would give the high chance of getting longest spectrum hole due to the Poisson arrival of PUs. In this regard, MRU always selects the longer spectrum hole than the other two strategies.

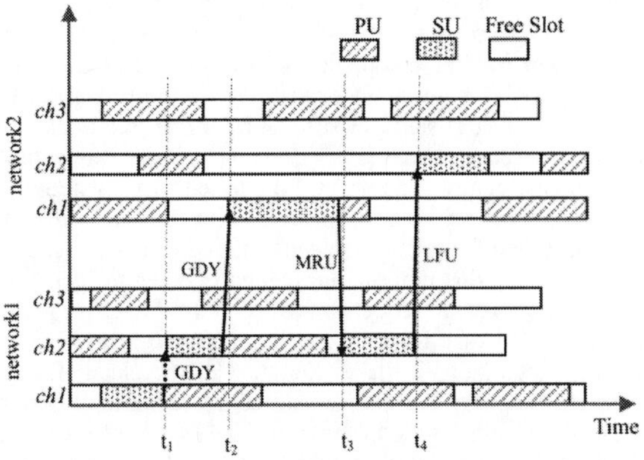

Figure 4. Spectrum mobility in CRNs

In Fig. 4, we have illustrated spectrum selection by a SU using these three strategies. At the time t_1 and t_2, the SU follows the GDY strategy to switch channel. At time t_1, the SU selects the spectrum hole of the first channel of *network1* even though channel 3 is also empty. Similarly, at time t_2, the SU selects the spectrum hole of the first channel of *network2*. At time t_3, the SU follows MRU strategy and selects the spectrum hole of channel 2 of *network1* as it is used most currently among the empty channels. At time t_4, the SU uses LFU strategy to switch to channel 2 of *network2* as the usage percentage of the channel by PU is less than other free channels.

C. CRAM Implementation in ns-3

We used the Time, Timer, Simulator, and RandomVariable classes to implement CRAM. The Time and Timer classes are used to schedule a task, such as assigning a channel to a SU/PU for a particular time interval and cancel it after completion of the task. The Simulator class is used for initial scheduling of the entire task in the simulation, i.e., it starts the PU and SU transmissions. The RandomVariable class is used to generate exponentially distributed random numbers. We used two schedulers: channel scheduler (Fig. 5) and SU scheduler (Fig. 6). The channel scheduler takes the mean value of λ_p and X_p as input. Following the distribution, the sequence generator generates a large number of sequences (over 1000). Each sequence consists of PU service time and duration of spectrum holes. During simulation, it makes the state of the channel either busy or free, based on the generated values. In the PU busy state, the channel scheduler starts the PU timer and makes the state as busy. After expiration of the PU timer, the free timer starts and the channel state becomes free. It would remain free up to the spectrum hole duration of the current sequence unless an SU sends a busy trigger. The SU busy trigger changes the channel state into busy state such that all SUs see that channel as busy. But, PU can interrupt the SU at any time and the SU has to move to another free channel or, pause state, if there is no free channel available. After expiration, it queries for the next sequence. A channel sensor database is implemented that acquires the channel information.

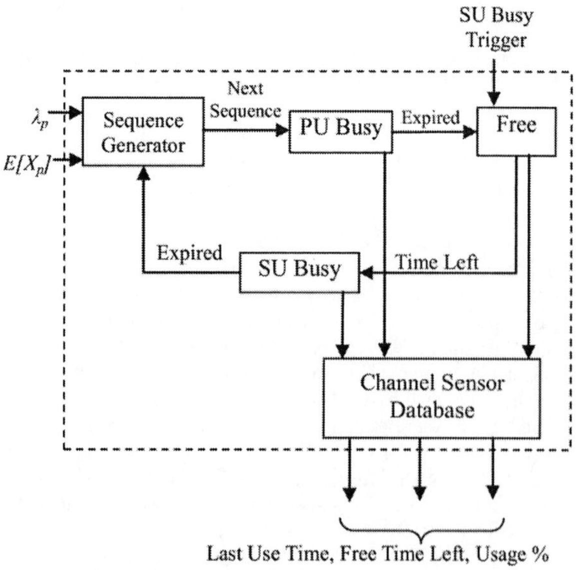

Figure 5. CRAM Channel Scheduler

In the SU scheduler, the user inputs its data transmission time and the spectrum selection strategy. The spectrum selection strategy acquires the channel information from all channels of all systems and makes a decision. It outputs the next channel number (k) and the remaining free time. If it gets the free time slot, it starts a transmission timer, giving a busy trigger to the kth channel scheduler. The start

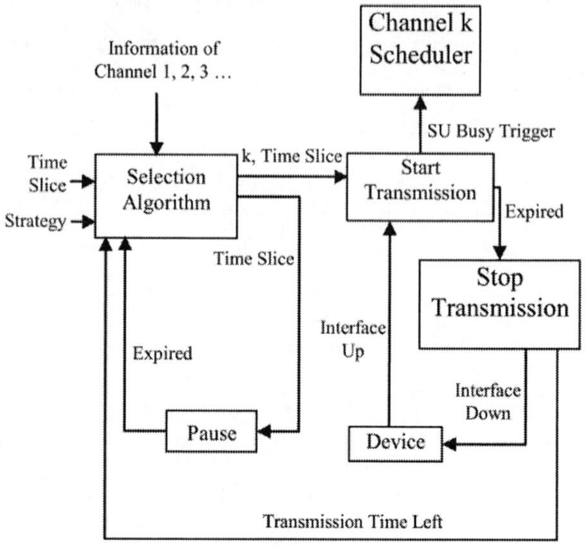

Figure 6. CRAM SU Scheduler

transmission functionality makes the SU's *network1* or, *network2* netdevice state into 'UP'. The Stop Transmission function makes the SU's corresponding state into 'Down' state. If at any point in time, the spectrum selection strategy cannot find a free channel, it pauses for a predefined timer value. After expiration of the pause timer, it again runs the spectrum selection strategy.

IV. MIPv6 Issues in CRNs

We have developed our own MIPv6 module [17] for ns-3 (as it is not available currently) on top of CRAM.

A. Simulation setup

We have considered two networks: *network1* and *network2* containing 20 and 10 channels respectively. The SU is opportunistic to *network2*. We used a constant position mobility model for the SUs because we are not interested in spatial mobility. We used λ_p = 1.5 and $E[N_s]$ = 4. Since multiple SUs are used, the contention among the SUs to access the same spectrum hole is managed through periodic sensing as shown in Fig. 2. It is to be noted that, for simplicity, we have measured the throughput performance of single SU. We used exponentially distributed connections with average connection length 480 bytes [25]. So, when the data rate of primary connection is 19.2 Kbps [25], we have $E[X_p]$= (480*8)/(19.2*10^3)=0.2 s. The Pause timeout value and spectrum handoff delay are set as 0.05 s and 0.01 s, respectively. The correspondent node (CN) and SU are running '*UDP Echo*' application and transferring packets at the rate of 80 Kbps. In this simulation, we keep the data rate fixed for all the PUs and the SUs. The whole simulation is run for 1000 s. However, we present only the results selected from 100 s. to 200 s. to highlight the design issues.

B. High RA Interval and Lifetime Period

1) Problem Description

If the duration of spectrum holes is very small, an SU may switch from one network (say *network2*) to another (say *network1*), reside there for a very short time, and then may return to *network2* again. When the SU switches to *network1*, the address configured in *network2* still remains valid for some more time. If it returns to *network2* quickly, it could use the previously configured CoA in *network2*, giving rise to two issues. *First*, when the SU is in *network1*, another SU in *network2* may configure the same CoA and execute DAD procedure. The DAD procedure detects the address as valid for obvious reasons. So, when the SU returns to *network2* quickly, duplicate addresses would exist in *network2* even if the DAD procedure detects no duplicity. So, the SU will use duplicate CoA in CRN if it makes a quick return in the old network. *Second*, the binding update and tunnel setup procedures in MIPv6 are always triggered after the completion of the DAD procedure. So, if the SU uses a previously configured CoA in *network2*, those procedures are skipped. Since MIPv6 is not triggered, the tunnel set up between the SU and its home agent (HA) would still be the older one and the traffic would not be redirected towards the SU. As a result, the performance of the SU degrades drastically.

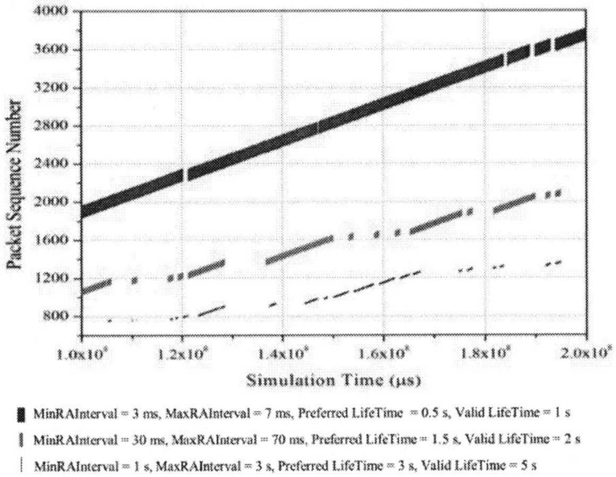

Figure 7. Behaviour under High RA and lifetime period in case of RA-based MIPv6

To illustrate the problem we have performed simulations for the RA-based and RS-based MIPv6 cases, but not for DHCP-based MIPv6, because DHCP eliminates the DAD period, and thus, does not suffer from this problem. In Fig. 7, we illustrate the impact of high RA interval and lifetime duration on packet flow in CRNs for RA-based MIPv6. First, we used MaxRAInterval=3 s and MinRAInterval=1 s as given in [14]. So, after switching back to *network1*, the SU does not perform MIPv6 operations for a long time due to high RA interval and lifetime period. This is evident from long gaps in packet sequence number in Fig. 7. Next, we decreased the values of the RA interval to MaxRAInterval=0.07 s and MinRAInterval=0.03 s. The corresponding simulation result (Fig. 7) shows that MIPv6 is unable to work gracefully, resulting in long gaps in packet sequence number. So, we further reduced the values of RA intervals to 7ms (MaxRAInterval) and 3ms (MinRAInterval), and then we found that all MIPv6 operations are completed successfully (Fig. 7). We also observed that, under this circumstance, a large number of control packets are being generated, leading to congestion. So, we argue that the *RA interval and lifetime period must be set considerably low in order to be appropriate for use in CRNs*.

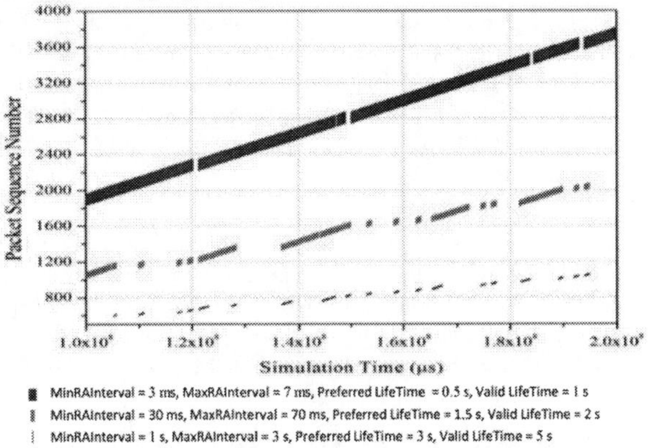

Figure 8. Behaviour under High RA and lifetime period in case of RS-based MIPv6

In Fig. 8, we illustrate that problem for RS-based MIPv6, taking the same set of values of RA interval and lifetime period. In this case, RS is sent by an SU after the link layer attachment and access point returns RA in response to RS. So, the RA delay is reduced but not completely eliminated. In this case, the SU receives RA more quickly than in the previous case. But, since the previously configured address still remains valid, the problem becomes more severe than RA-based MIPv6. The difference is seen in case of RA interval between 1-3 s. Comparing Figs. 7 and 8, we observe that there are more gaps in packet sequence number in RS-based MIPv6 than that in RA-based MIPv6. So, RS-based MIPv6, which actually reduces handoff delay, degrades performance much more than RA-based MIPv6 does. However, this difference is not seen in cases of small RA intervals like 30-70 ms and 3-7 ms, as the RA interval and RS delay are almost the same in these cases.

TABLE II. MIPV6 HANDOFF PARAMETERS

Parameter	Meaning	Parameter	Meaning
R_M	Max RA Interval	R_m	Min RA Interval
R_A	RA Delay	T_{VL}	IPv6 Address Valid Lifetime
T_{DHCP}	DHCP address acquisition delay	R_S	RS Delay
τ	Wireless hop delay	T_{BU}	BU Delay
T_{DAD}	DAD period	T_{SH}	Spectrum handoff delay
T_L	Link layer attachment delay		

2) Validation with the Numerical Results

To validate the '*MIPv6 not triggered*' problem, we use the MIPv6 handoff parameters given in Table II. The timing diagram, shown in Fig. 9, presents the timing of RA message reception by the SU and the behavior of address expiry timer in case of RA-based MIPv6. After getting RA in *network2*, the SU switches to *network1* following a spectrum handoff and returns back to *network2* that provides the RA message again. The address expiry timer is last updated when the SU receives the RA message before switching to *network1*, as indicated in Fig. 9. After switching back to network2, the old address, previously configured in network2, is not expired and the SU uses that address without configuring a new address Hence, DAD is not performed and MIPv6 is not triggered. After getting RA in *network2* again, the life time timer will be updated again. So, the total time elapsed between these two updates is $2R_A + \frac{W}{2} + 2T_{SH}$. Here, we assume the spectrum hole duration as $W/2$, instead of W, because the SU acquires the spectrum hole randomly in between 0 to W interval. The '*MIPv6 not triggered*' problem happens if the valid lifetime is greater than the elapsed time between two updates in *network2*. So, the probability of the problem can be calculated as follows:

$$T_{VL} > 2R_A + \frac{W}{2} + 2T_{SH} = P(W < 2(T_{VL} - 2R_A - 2T_{SH})) \quad (13)$$

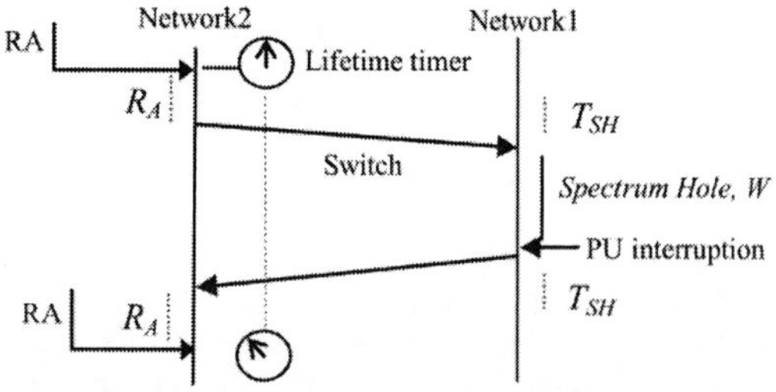

Figure 9. Timing diagram for RA-based MIPv6

In the previous case, if the SU continues in *network1*, even after PU interrupt, due to channel unavailability in *network2*, then the stay time in *network1* will increase. For two such PU interruptions, the spectrum hole value would be $2*W/2$. So if the SU returns to *network2* after 'n' PU interrupts in *network1*, then the probability of '*MIPv6 not triggered*' problem would be:

$$P\left(T_{VL} > 2R_A + n*\frac{W}{2} + (n+1)T_{SH}\right)$$
$$= P\left(W < (\frac{2}{n})*(T_{VL} - 2R_A - (n+1)T_{SH})\right) \quad (14)$$
$$= P\left(W < \frac{L}{n}\right)$$

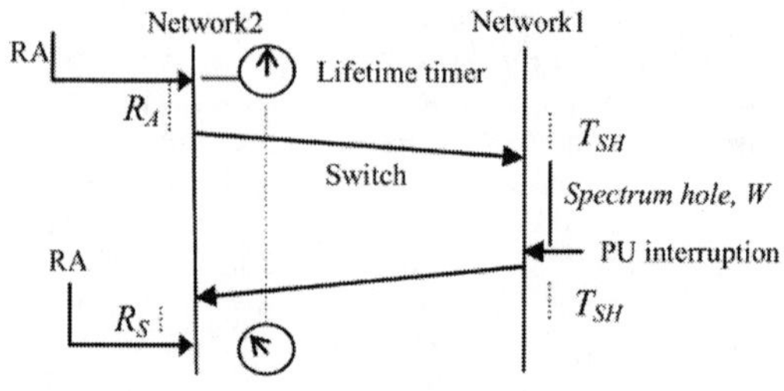

Figure 10. Timing diagram for RS-based MIPv6

where $L = 2(T_{VL} - 2R_A - (n+1)T_{SH})$ is a constant. Using the state transition diagram, shown in Fig. 3, the total probability of '*MIPv6 not triggered*' problem can be calculated as follows:

$$P(MIPv6\_Not\_Triggered) = \sum_{n=1}^{\infty} f(W < \frac{L}{n}) * \left(\rho_2^{C2}\left(1-\rho_1^{C1}\right)\right)^{n-1} * \left(1-\rho_2^{C2}\right) \quad (15)$$

where $f\left(W < (\frac{2}{n})*L\right)$ can be calculated from (12) as follows:

$$f\left(W < \frac{L}{n}\right) = \int_0^{\frac{L}{n}} f(W = t)$$
$$= \int_0^{\frac{L}{n}} \frac{\lambda_p \mu_p}{\lambda_p + \mu_p} e^{-t\lambda_p} dt \quad (16)$$
$$= \frac{\mu_p}{\lambda_p + \mu_p}\left(1 - e^{-(\frac{L}{n})\lambda_p}\right)$$

It is to be noted that the RA delay depends upon the RA intervals set by the AR and the attachment timing of the SU to the new link. As given in [26], R_A can be given as follows:

$$R_A = \frac{R_M^2 + R_M R_m + R_m^2}{3(R_M + R_m)} \quad (17)$$

The timing diagram for RS-based MIPv6 is shown in Fig. 10. The SU receives RA quickly after switching to *network2*. The probability of '*MIPv6 not triggered*" problem, if the SU returns to *network2* after 'n' PU interrupts in *network1*, would be as follows:

$$P\left(T_{VL} > R_A + R_S + n * \frac{W}{2} + (n+1)T_{SH}\right) = P\left(W < (\frac{2}{n}) * (T_{VL} - R_A - R_S - (n+1)T_{SH})\right) \quad (18)$$

It is to be noted that the RS delay is two times the wireless hop delay, i.e., $R_s = 2*\tau$. The total probability of '*MIPv6 not triggered*' problem can be computed in the similar way as in (15).

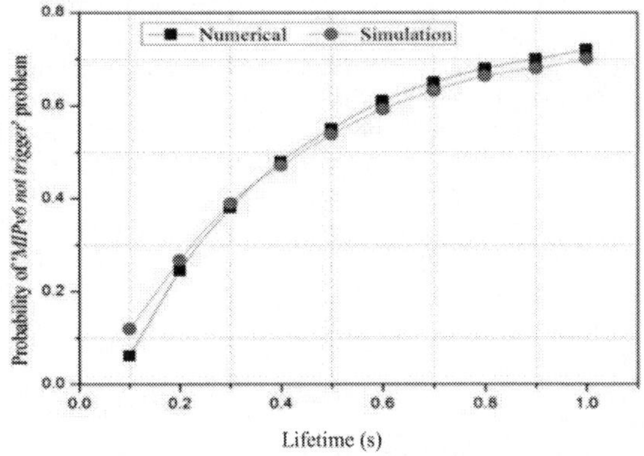

Figure 11. Validation graph for "MIPv6 not triggered" problem in RA-based MIPv6

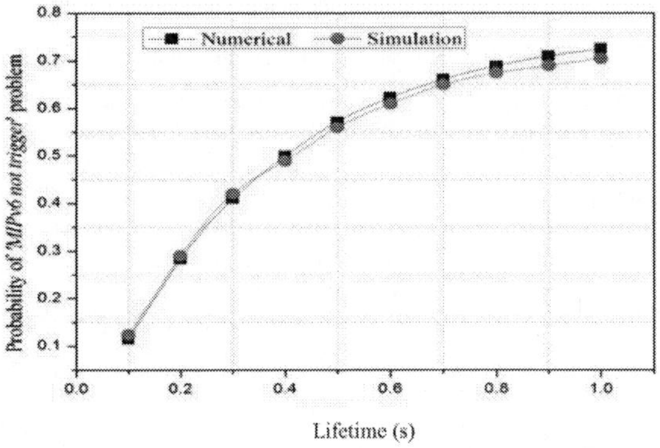

Figure 12. Validation graph for "MIPv6 not triggered" problem in RS-based MIPv6

The validation graphs for RA-based and RS-based MIPv6 are shown in Fig. 11 and Fig. 12, respectively. Taking τ=0.1 ms, R_m=30 ms, and R_M=70 ms, we vary T_{VL} to obtain the total probability of occurrence of '*MIPv6 not triggered*' problem. In our simulation, we find this probability by counting occurrences of the problem and dividing it by the total number of switches from *network1* to *network2*. It is to be noted that the chance of occurrence of the problem will increase if W in *network1* is less than T_{VL} in *network2*. The time of stay of SU in *network1* mainly depends on W, which is an exponential variable with mean 0.52 s, computed using (12). So, if T_{VL} is increased from 0 to the mean of W, there is a sharp increase in the probability due to the increase in the number of spectrum holes. For T_{VL}=0.52 s to T_{VL}=1.0 s, there are fewer cases where W lies between mean of W and T_{VL}. First, the frequency of spectrum holes decreases after the mean due to its exponential property. Second, the stay time of SU in *network1* depends on the number of PU interruptions and the probability of high PU interruptions is small, as indicated in (15). So, the rate of increase in probability is slow in this period. It is to be noted that, in both graphs, the numerical results almost match with the simulation results, which validates our simulation work.

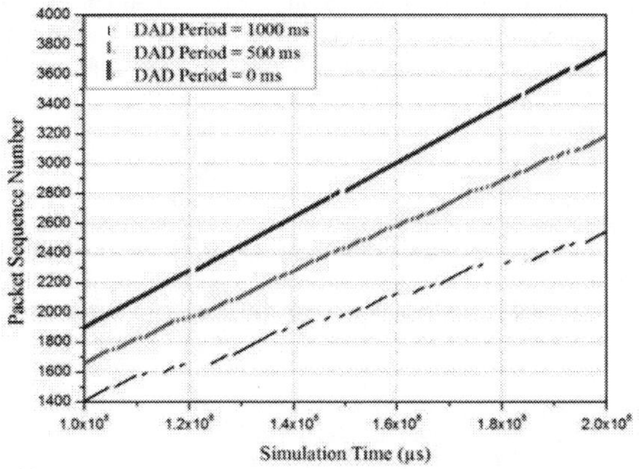

Figure 13. Behaviour of RA-based MIPv6 under High DAD period

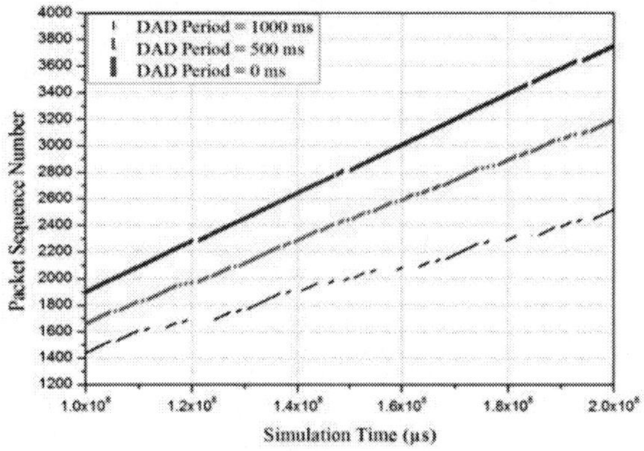

Figure 14. Behaviour of RS-based MIPv6 under High DAD period

C. High DAD Period

1) Problem Description

RFC 6275 [9] has mentioned the default DAD period as 1 s, which may be higher than the considered duration of spectrum holes in CRNs. Whenever an SU switches to a new network, the address configuration procedure – in particular, the DAD procedure – consumes almost the entire spectrum hole, and hence, the spectrum hole cannot be used for data transmission at all (Fig. 13 and Fig. 14). So, the throughput of SUs degrades in CRNs. For this reason, the DAD period must also be reduced to make MIPv6 more effective in CRNs.

2) Validation with the Numerical Results

The RA-based MIPv6 handoff delay can be given as follows,

$$T_{HO} = T_L + R_A + T_{DAD} + T_{BU} \qquad (19)$$

For the successful completion of the MIPv6 handoff process, the handoff delay must be less than the spectrum hole value. So the '*incomplete IP handoff*' problem for one PU interruption happens if the condition, $W/2 < T_L+R_A+T_{DAD}+T_{BU}$ holds. For '*n*' PU interruptions, the probability of occurrence of '*incomplete IP handoff*' problem would be:

$$P((n/2)*W < T_{HO}) = P(W < (2/n)*T_{HO}) \qquad (20)$$

Assuming, $S=2*T_{HO}$, we can compute the total probability of '*incomplete IP handoff*' problem using (15), by replacing *L* by *S*. In case of RS-based MIPv6, R_A is to be replaced by R_S in (19). The total probability can be computed in the similar way as given in (15).

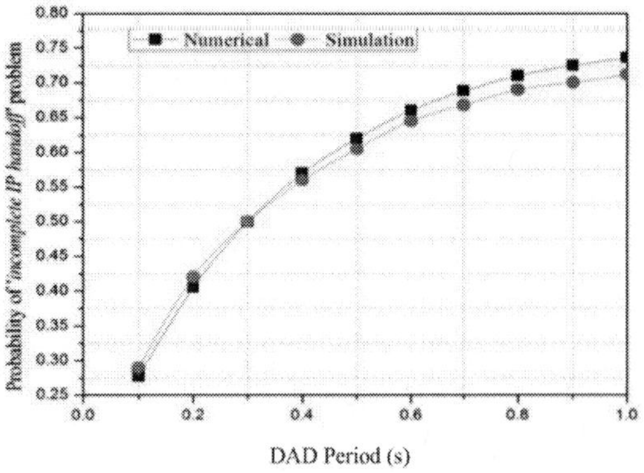

Figure 15. Validation graph for "incomplete IP handoff" problem in RA-based MIPv6

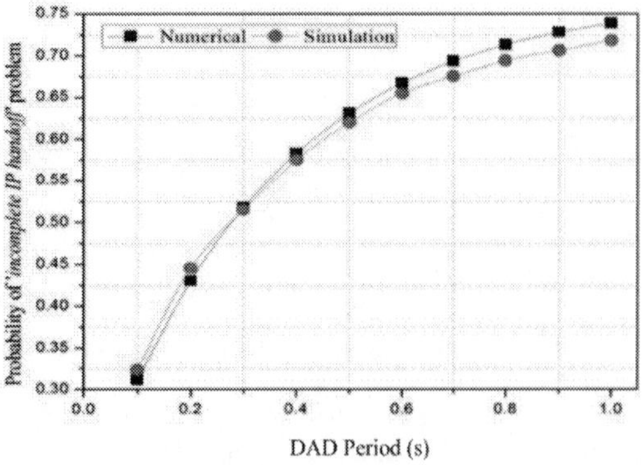

Figure 16. Validation graph for "incomplete IP handoff" problem in RS-based MIPv6

The validation graphs for '*incomplete IP handoff*' problem are shown in Fig. 15 and Fig. 16 in the case of RA-based and RS-based MIPv6, respectively. Taking T_L=10 ms and T_{BU}=23 ms, we vary T_{DAD} to obtain the total probability of occurrence of '*incomplete IP handoff*' problem in *network1*. The '*incomplete IP handoff*' problem occurs if the IP handoff delay is higher than the spectrum hole duration. It is known that T_{DAD} is the dominant delay component in the IP handoff delay. So, the chance of the problem will increase if we increase T_{DAD}. We observed that the frequency of *W* in *network1* is high but with small spectrum hole durations for T_{DAD}=0 to T_{DAD}=0.52 s. due to its exponential nature. So, with increase in T_{DAD} from 0 to 0.52 s, the probability of occurrence of the problem increases sharply. Also due to the exponential nature of *W*, for T_{DAD}= 0.52 s to T_{DAD}=1.0 s, the frequency of *W* is reduced with small spectrum hole duration. So, the rate of increase in the probability is slow in this period. It is to be noted that the numerical results nearly match with the simulation results, thereby validating the correctness of our simulation.

TABLE III. SIMULATION PARAMETER VALUES

Variable Parameter	Other Parameter Values
λ_p	$(E[X_P])_{LOW}$=0.1, $(E[X_P])_{HIGH}$=0.3, $E[N_S]$=4
$E[X_p]$	$(\lambda_p)_{LOW}$=1, $(\lambda_p)_{HIGH}$=1.5, $E[N_S]$=4
$E[N_S]$	$(\lambda_p)_{LOW}$=2.0, $(\lambda_p)_{HIGH}$=2.5, $(E[X_P])_{LOW}$=0.1, $(E[X_P])_{HIGH}$=0.3

V. ANALYSIS OF THE IMPACT OF SPECTRUM MOBILITY

In this section, we present the main results and discuss their implications at length. Here, we have made some minor changes in the simulation setup used in Section IV-A, in order to bring in more randomness in the availability of spectrum holes. The channels of CRAM are characterized as either of high usage or of low usage, to benefit from LFU and MRU strategies. We have used λ_p, $E[X_p]$, and $E[N_s]$ variables to control the emptiness of the channels (Table III). Also, to alleviate the problems explained in Section IV, we have taken 7 ms and 3 ms for MaxRAInterval and MinRAInterval, respectively. The preferred lifetime values are assumed to be 0.5 s and 1 s, respectively. The simulation has been performed for RA-based and DHCP-based MIPv6 only, and not for RS-based MIPv6. This is because, for small RA intervals, RS-based MIPv6 behaves almost similarly as RA-based MIPv6 does.

We have randomly assigned either $E[X_p]_{HIGH}$ or $E[X_p]_{LOW}$ values in all 30 channels, while keeping $E[N_s]$=4. Increasing λ_p increases the frequency of spectrum holes but with reduced duration of each. From Fig. 17, we observe that, up to $\lambda_p \le 2.8$, the number of IP handoffs increases sub-linearly, and, for $\lambda_p > 2.8$, the frequency drops abruptly. So PU arrival rate of 3 per s acts as a kind of threshold for this experimental setting. We note that, for $0.1 \le \lambda_p \le 2.2$, all IP handoffs are completed successfully due to sufficiently large spans of the spectrum holes. As a result, the throughput of the SU is reduced only slightly (this reduction is primarily due to the lengthy handoff operation of MIPv6) as shown in

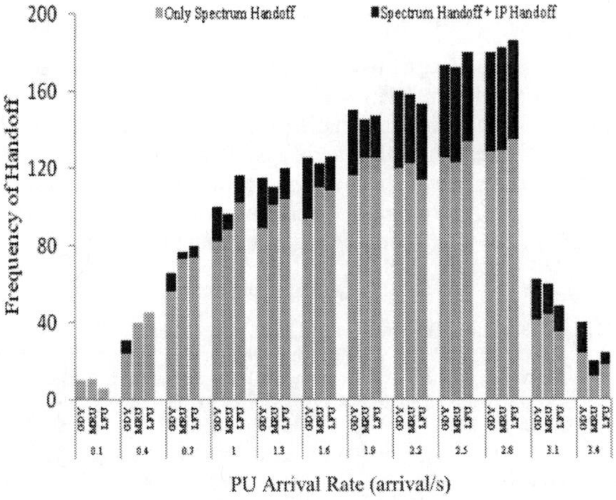

Figure 17. Variation of IP handoff with PU arrival rate

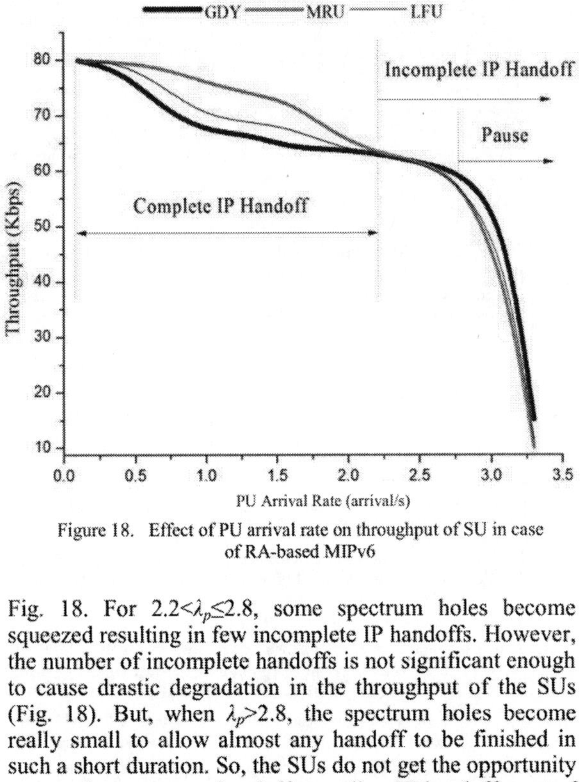

Figure 18. Effect of PU arrival rate on throughput of SU in case of RA-based MIPv6

Fig. 18. For $2.2<\lambda_p\leq2.8$, some spectrum holes become squeezed resulting in few incomplete IP handoffs. However, the number of incomplete handoffs is not significant enough to cause drastic degradation in the throughput of the SUs (Fig. 18). But, when $\lambda_p>2.8$, the spectrum holes become really small to allow almost any handoff to be finished in such a short duration. So, the SUs do not get the opportunity to complete spectrum handoff as well as IP handoff most of the time. In this case, the SUs cycle between pause and channel sensing phases (Fig. 2), thereby reducing the throughput of the SUs drastically (Fig. 18). However, in the case of DHCP-based MIPv6, incomplete IP handoff does not occur at all because DAD process is not used; as a result, there is no sharp degradation of throughput initially (Fig. 19). But, beyond $\lambda_p=2.2$, the holes become too small to allow completion of handoff; SUs start to cycle between

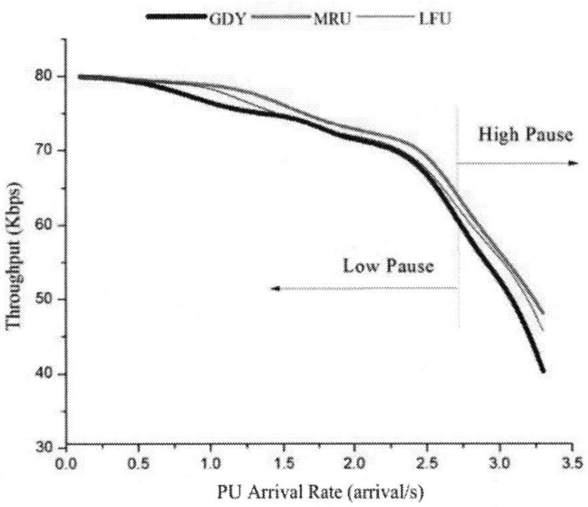

Figure 19. Effect of PU arrival rate on throughput of SU in DHCP-based MIPv6

pause and channel sensing phases (Fig. 2); so there is a gradual degradation of throughput performance (Fig. 19). Comparatively, DHCP-based MIPv6 performs better than the other two versions do, implying that the former could be a better choice in CRNs.

Now, we focus our attention to the selection strategies (different colors in Figs. 18 and 19 indicate them). Fig. 18 shows that, for $\lambda_p\leq2.2$, the MRU strategy performs better than LFU and GDY strategies. This is because the MRU strategy always finds those free channels, which can be used for a longer period of time without needing to perform another IP handoff shortly. That is not true for the other two strategies. However, when $\lambda_p>2.2$, the average spectrum hole duration becomes very small and is entirely consumed by the MIPv6 handoff procedure in all the three spectrum selection strategies. So, all three performs equally bad then. Since MRU always selects the longest spectrum hole, it wastes more time than other two strategies in RA-based MIPv6 (Fig. 18). However, in case of DHCP-based MIPv6, wastage of spectrum hole due to MIPv6 handoff operation is reduced. Hence, MRU strategy performs better than LFU and GDY do (Fig. 19).

For $0.1\leq E[X_p]\leq0.4$, the number of IP handoffs is increasing. In particular, for $0.1\leq E[X_p]\leq0.3$, all IP handoffs are completed successfully, leading to minor throughput degradation largely due to lengthy MIPv6 handoff operation only (Fig. 20). But, for $0.3<E[X_p]\leq0.4$, most of the IP handoffs are incomplete. As a result, the throughput of the SUs drops quickly (Fig. 21). Also, when $E[X_p]>0.4$, the number of IP handoffs itself is reduced because the SUs are mostly cycling between channel sensing and pause phases (Fig. 2). As a result, the throughput of the SUs degrades sharply (Fig. 20). In DHCP-based MIPv6, for $E[X_p]<0.4$, all IP handoffs are successfully completed due to elimination of T_{DAD}. But, for $E[X_p]>0.4$, the SUs are unable to find spectrum holes and cycles between channel sensing and

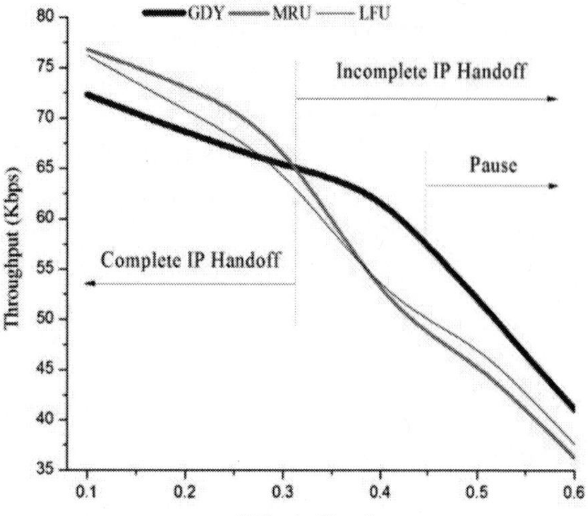

Figure 20. Impact of PU service time on throughput of SU in case of RA-based MIPv6

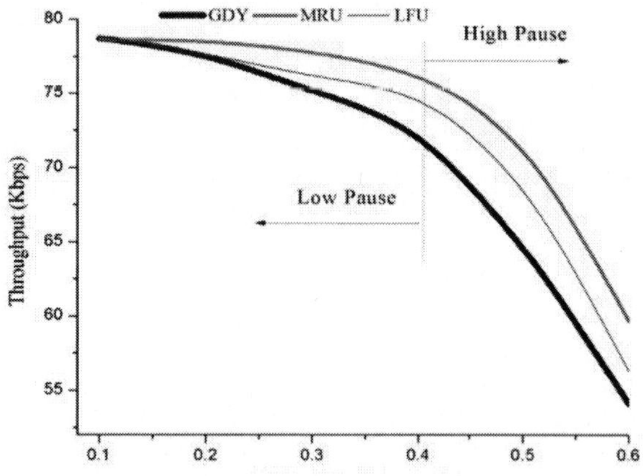

Figure 21. Impact of PU service time on throughput of SU in DHCP-based MIPv6

pause phases, and hence, there is a sharp degradation of throughput in this region (Fig. 21).

VI. Conclusion And Future Work

We have analyzed the number of IP handoffs resulting from spectrum mobility in the absence of spatial mobility. Our study has carried out a root-cause analysis of the observation that MIPv6 cannot work properly in CRNs, and reveals that it is due to high values of RA interval, lifetime period of CoA, and DAD period. That is why the performance of MIPv6 degrades considerably especially when the spectrum holes are becoming smaller with more PUs turning active at a higher rate. So, our first recommendation is that the values for these parameters must be reduced to appropriate levels for possible use of MIPv6 in CRNs.

Our second conclusion is that, for lower values of PU traffic parameters, MRU and LFU have better performance than GDY has; but, for higher values of those parameters, GDY is better than MRU and LFU. Our future work includes design a dynamic spectrum selection strategy to fit with MIPv6 for heterogeneous spectrum mobility scenarios in CRNs in order to improve the throughput of SUs further.

References

[1] M. K. Rana, B. Sardar, S. Mandal, and D. Saha, "Analyzing the Effect of Spectrum Mobility on Mobile IPv6 in Cognitive Radio Networks," The Sixth International Conference on Advances in Cognitive Radio (COCORA 2016), IARIA, February 2016, pp. 26-32, ISSN: 2308-4251, ISBN: 978-1-61208-456-5.

[2] B. Al-Mubarak, "WiFi for UAE Mobile Service Providers: Offloading Mobile Data Traffic to Wi-Fi Can Save UAE Operators up to US$316 Million," Cisco Internet Business Solutions Group (IBSG), Cisco, January 2013.

[3] K. Patil, R. Prasad, and K. Skouby, "A Survey of Worldwide Spectrum Occupancy Measurement Campaigns for Cognitive Radio," Devices and Communications (ICDeCom), International Conference on, Mesra, 2011, pp. 1-5, doi: 10.1109/ICDECOM.2011.5738472.

[4] S. Buljore, H. Harada, S. Filin, and V. Ivanov, "Architecture and Enablers for optimized Radio Resource Usage in Heterogeneous Wireless Access Networks: The IEEE 1900.4 working group," IEEE Communications Magazine, vol. 47, no. 1, pp. 122-129, January 2009.

[5] ETSI - European Telecommunications Standards Institute, Retrieved from http://www.etsi.org/, July 2016.

[6] ITU-R, RadioCommunication sector of ITU, "Introduction of CR systems in the Wireless World-Research Achievements and Future Challenges for End-to-End Efficiency," Report ITU-R M.2330-0, November 2014.

[7] I. Christian, S. Moh, I. Chung, and J. Lee, "Spectrum mobility in cognitive radio networks," IEEE Communications Magazine, vol. 50, June 2012, pp. 114 – 121.

[8] G. Wu, M. Mizuno, and P. J.M. Havinga, "MIRAI architecture for heterogeneous network," IEEE Communications Magazine, vol. 40, no. 2, February 2002, pp. 126-134, doi=http://dx.doi.org/10.1109/35.983919.

[9] C. Perkins, D. Johnson, and J. Arkko, "Mobility support in IPv6," RFC 6275, IETF, 2011.

[10] M. Kataoka, T. Ishikawa, S. Hanaoka, M. Yano, and S. Nishimura, "Evaluation of inter base station handover for cognitive radio," Proceeding on IEEE Radio and Wireless Symposium, January 2008, pp. 251-254.

[11] Y. S. Chen and J. S. Hong, "A Relay-Assisted Protocol for Spectrum Mobility and Handover in Cognitive LTE Networks," in IEEE Systems Journal, vol. 7, no. 1, pp. 77-91, March 2013.

[12] J. F. Weng, B. H. Ku, J. C. Chen, and W. T. Chen, "Channel holding time of packet sessions in all-IP cellular networks", Proc. IEEE ICPADS, December 2014, pp. 404-411.

[13] M. Hoyhtya, J. Lehtomaki, J. Kokkoniemi, M. Matinmikko, and A. Mammela, "Measurements and analysis of spectrum occupancy with several bandwidths," IEEE International Conference on Communications (ICC, 2013), Budapest, 2013, pp. 4682-4686, doi: 10.1109/ICC.2013.6655311.

[14] J. Seob Lee, S. J. Koh, and S. H. Kim, "Analysis of handoff delay for Mobile IPv6," Vehicular Technology Conference (VTC2004), IEEE 60th, Vol. 4, 2004, pp. 2967-2969.

[15] R. Droms, J. Bound, T. Lemon, C. Perkins, and M. Carney, "Dynamic Host Configuration Protocol for IPv6 (DHCPv6)," RFC 3315, IETF, 2003.

[16] Network simulator (ns), version 3, Retrieved from http://www.nsnam.org/, January 2016.

[17] M. K. Rana, B. Sardar, S. Mandal, and D. Saha, "Implementation and performance evaluation of a mobile IPv6 (MIPv6) simulation model for ns-3," Simulation Modelling Practice and Theory, Volume 72, March 2017, pp. 1-22, ISSN 1569-190X, http://dx.doi.org/10.1016/j.simpat.2016.12.005.

[18] L. C. Wang, C. W. Wang, and C. J. Chang, "Optimal target channel sequence for multiple spectrum handoffs in cognitive radio networks," IEEE Transactions on Communication," vol. 60, September 2012, pp. 2444-2455.

[19] L.-C. Wang, C.-W. Wang, and C.-J. Chang, "Modeling and Analysis for Spectrum Handoffs in Cognitive Radio Networks," IEEE Transactions on Mobile Computing," vol. 11, July 2012, pp. 1499-1513.

[20] R. Southwell, J. Huang, and X. Liu, "Spectrum mobility games," INFOCOM, 2012 Proceedings IEEE, March 2012, pp. 37-45.

[21] J. Sztrik, "Basic queueing theory," University of Debrecen, Faculty of Informatics, 2011.

[22] C. W. Wang, L. C. Wang, and Adachi F., "Modeling and Analysis for Reactive-Decision Spectrum Handoff in Cognitive Radio Networks," Proceedings IEEE Global Telecommunications Conference (GLOBECOM 2010), December 2010, pp. 1-6.

[23] S. U. Yoon, and E. Ekici, "Voluntary Spectrum Handoff: A Novel Approach to Spectrum Management in CRNs," IEEE International Conference on Communications (ICC), May 2010, pp. 1-5, 23-27.

[24] G. Yuan, R. C. G.rammenos, Y. Yang, and W. Wang, "Performance Analysis of Selective Opportunistic Spectrum Access With Traffic Prediction," IEEE Transactions on Vehicular Technology, vol. 59, no. 4, May 2010, pp. 1949-1959.

[25] ETSI, "Universal Mobile Telecommunications System (UMTS): Selection Procedures for the Choice of Radio Transmission Technologies of the UMTS," Technical Report UMTS 30.03, version 3.2.0, April 1998.

[26] Y. H. Han, and S. H. Hwang, "Movement detection analysis in mobile IPv6," IEEE Communications Letters, January, 2006, pp. 59-61, doi: 10.1109/LCOMM.2006.1576570.

International Journal on Advances in Telecommunications, vol 9 no 3 & 4, year 2016, http://www.iariajournals.org/telecommunications/

Modelling and Prioritization of System Risks in Early Project Phases

Mohammad Rajabalinejad
Faculty of Engineering Technology, University of Twente, Enschede, the Netherlands
M.Rajabalinejad@utwente.nl

Abstract--**The rising complexity of product and systems demands further attention to potential Risks. While researchers explore tools and methods to identify system risk, its prioritization remains a challenging task in a multi-stakeholder environment. Hazard is the source of risk and causes harm. Harm may have different degree of severity. Next to the degree of severity, frequency of its occurrence is relevant to risk. These are often hardly quantifiable. While the accurate quantification remains a challenge, a flexible and pluralistic approach can bring major risks on the top of list. This paper offers a methodology for ranking risks in early phases of design with presence of a high level of uncertainty. It uses a pluralistic approach for prioritization of hazards. It adapts probability theory to embed flexibly in communication with stakeholders and process the available information. A graphical tool facilitates this communication and probabilistically utilize available information about system hazards. It suggests the "degree of consensus" as a metric to rank the identified risks. This metric represents the consent of stakeholders on the system risks used for system architecture, design decisions, or alternative evaluations. The paper explains the mathematical formulation and presents an application example for this.**

Keywords - consensus; risk; severity; occurrence; uncertainty; prioritization; ranking.

I. Introduction

A. *Risk and hazard*

Hazards are the risk sources, and their proper recognition and prioritization leads to a better understanding of risks and their management. The rising complexity and cross-disciplinary nature of systems demands further development for identification of hazards [1, 2]. Hazard is the potential source of harm [3], and this creates a direct link between hazard and risk. If a hazard is not identified, risks remain unattended.

The European norm on risk assessment [4] summaries the tools and methods applicable to hazard identification in categories of strongly applicable and applicable. The strongly applicable methods for risk identifications are brainstorming, Delphi, Check-lists, Primary hazard analysis, Hazard and operability studies (HAZOP), Environmental risk assessment, SWIFT, Scenario analysis (SA), Failure mode and effect analysis (FMEA), Cause-and-effect analysis, Human reliability analysis (HRA), Reliability centered maintenance (RCM), Consequence/probability matrix. The applicable methods for hazard identifications are Business impact analysis (BIA), Fault tree analysis (FTA), Event tree analysis (ETA), Cause and consequence analysis (CCA), Layer protection analysis, Sneak circuit analysis, Markov analysis, FN curves, Risk indices, cost/benefit analysis, and Multi-criteria decision analysis.

After recognition of a hazard, severity of its harm and probability of its occurrence is needed to estimate the risk as shown in the figure below.

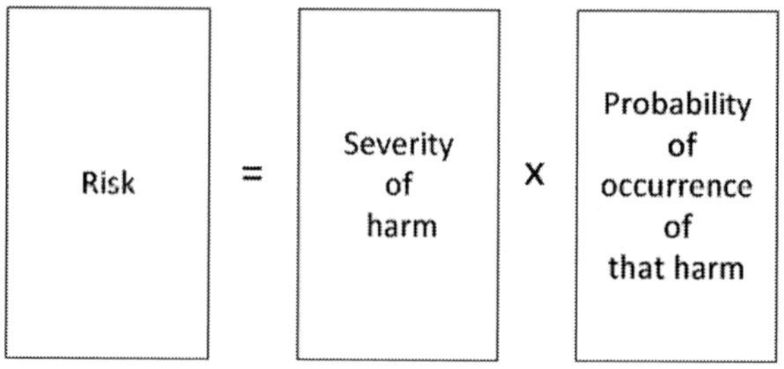

Figure 1. Risk is a function of severity of harm and probability of occurrence of that harm [4].

Next sections in the paper highlights the importance of risk and uncertainty recognition in early project phase, the involvement of stakeholders for elicitation, and the influence of hazards on system requirements. Thereafter, the paper discusses an approach for the modelling and communication for system risks. As hazard is the source of risk, terms hazards and risks are interchangeably used in the context of this paper.

B. *Risk and uncertainty*

There are always many factors and influences which can make it uncertain whether the project achieves its objectives. This uncertainty in early project phases is very high as discussed in details in [5]. Besides, the complexity of projects intensifies this uncertainty as shown in Figure 2. This uncertainty imposes risk on the project, and the mitigation of this risk is easier in early project phase. Figure 2 shows that the cost of risk mitigation increases as the project further develops. In order to manage this risk, the first step is its identification, then analysis, evaluation, and then taking appropriate measurements.

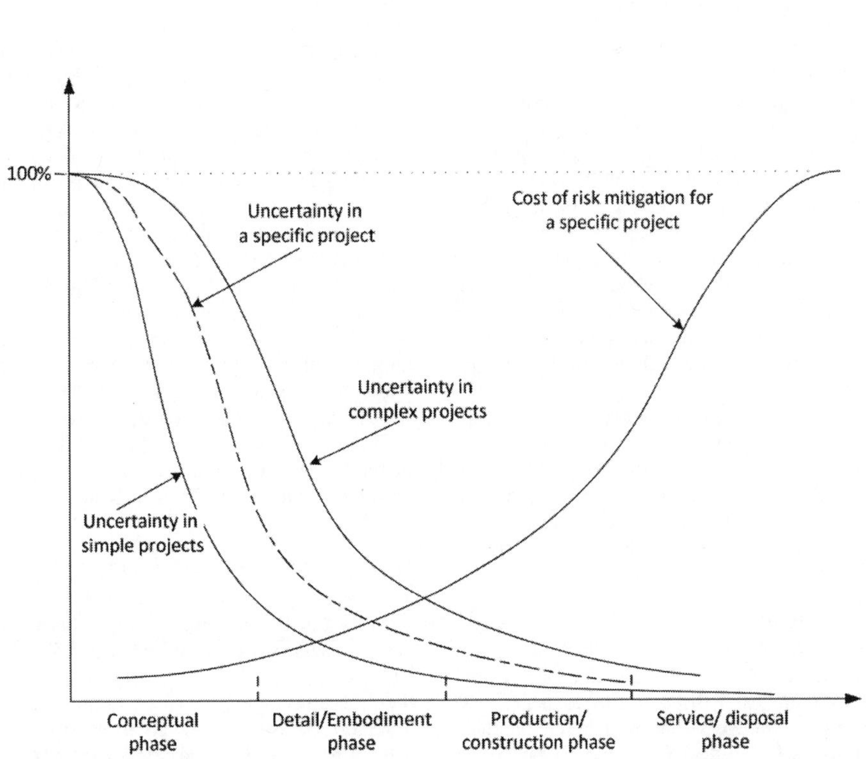

Figure 2. This figure highlights the presence of uncertainty and risk in the course of a full project life-cycle (adapted from [5]).

In early project phases, proper actions against risk factors, results in many competitor advantages including but not limited to the following (see [6]):

- higher likelihood for success
- encouraging the proactive measurements against risk factors
- higher stakeholder confidence and trust
- identification of opportunities and treats
- more effective use of resources against risk factors

To properly identify project risks and progress in the project, useful information is required. This information reduces uncertainties, increases utilities, and creates value for the system. This is because useful information for a designer leads to better design choices that ultimately influence the rest of design including concept, details, or services. This quest, however, may result in information overwhelming, and a design team may be exposed to a lot of information that hinders focusing on the key aspects. In system design with the multi-stakeholder nature of systems, divergent expectations of stakeholders can prevent a designer to focus on the key drivers for a system design.

In an interdisciplinary system, there are a lot of mono- or multi- disciplinary hazards that are hard to quantify or prioritize. Quantification of hazards in the form of frequency of occurrence or severity comes after its realization. Furthermore, this quantification may be subject to change over time.

Lack of proper hazard identification or prioritization leads to rising complexity in the risk analysis and management. Most of the currently applied hazard identification methods result in a hazard pool. In such a view, a larger system results a larger hazard pool which makes the prioritization more complex. The next section discusses this in further details.

C. *System hazards and requirements*

A good understanding of hazards and risks helps developing a proper list of (safety) requirements. The importance of requirements have been discussed in design literatures, see e.g. [7]. This study adapts a pluralistic approach for highlighting system hazards, risks or requirements.

Literatures have discussed that many engineering design methods pay attention to system risks when there is already a concept for the system. Yet proper view of main hazards helps forming an architecture that fits better to them [8, 9]. Recognition of system hazards is indeed a pluralistic approach, and the design team/ architecture need to approach different system stakeholders and explore their concerns about the system risks and hazards. Stakeholder in this paper is used as a general term that includes system shareholders, users, designers, experts and etcetera, and the concern refers to a stakeholder concern including the specific hazard.

Literatures confirm that an incomplete set of stakeholders may lead to incomplete results since there are problems arising from the scope, understanding and validation of needs, concerns or concern [10, 11] in the course of communication with stakeholders. Therefore, identification of stakeholders and elicitation of information are considered as prerequisites for understanding the system hazards. Systems often involves a large number of stakeholders [12]. Figure 3 presents the functional diagram for identifying stakeholders and communicating with them. This results in a pool of hazards with a lot of information [see [1]]. Ranking of this information helps the designer to keep her focus on the key aspects. Recognition of key hazards is likely to be seen subjectively as different stakeholders tend to focus on their areas of interest and pay more attention to the hazards that influence their interest.

This study builds on the previous study [1] on ranking system hazards and suggests ranking of system risks based on two measures of severity and occurrence through a pluralistic approach. It therefore focuses to offer a pluralistic approach that communicates well with stakeholders, provides freedom for presenting the opinions, and embraces doubts or uncertainties in their information.

D. *Ranking of system hazards*

This study builds on the assumption that key hazards in design are recognized by the consensus of stakeholders, and they can be rated systematically through a ranking process. In general, ranking of parameters (hazards) based on their importance is well discussed in decision models. The use of multi criteria decision models typically involves a systematic ranking process as for instance indicated in [13, 14]. The influence of the ranking process on final decisions is for example explained in [15]. A review of subjective ranking methods shows that different methods cannot guarantee accurate results. This inconsistency in judgment explains difficulty of assigning reliable and subjective weights to the requirements. A systematic approach for ranking is described in [16] that is a generalization of Saaty's pairwise structure [17]. Given the presence of subjectivity in the ranking process, sensitivity analysis of the design criteria is used to study the influence of variation and the ranking process on the decisions made [18]. Furthermore, some approaches e.g. the task-oriented weighing approach is effectively used. This approach is meant to limit the subjectivity of criteria weighting [19]. It suggests an algorithm to rank criteria objectively while considering the uncertainty in criteria weight [20]. The approach is based on introducing fuzzy numbers that imposes specified membership functions, which has been also used in [21, 22].

The methods used to identify the system hazards are mentioned earlier in this paper. The outlines of these methods are available elsewhere in for example [6]. The use of these methods results in a bank of information called a "pool of hazards".

E. *Pool of hazards; severity, occurrence and risk*

The so called pool of hazards integrates the identified hazards that threaten the system. This pool includes all the system hazards recognized by stakeholders. As the pool can become of enormous size, a method is required for listing them based on their priorities. Figure 4 schematically shows a set of hazards recognized for a system. For ranking the system hazards, this study uses two metrics of frequency of occurrence and degree of severity. These metrics are further described in the next sections.

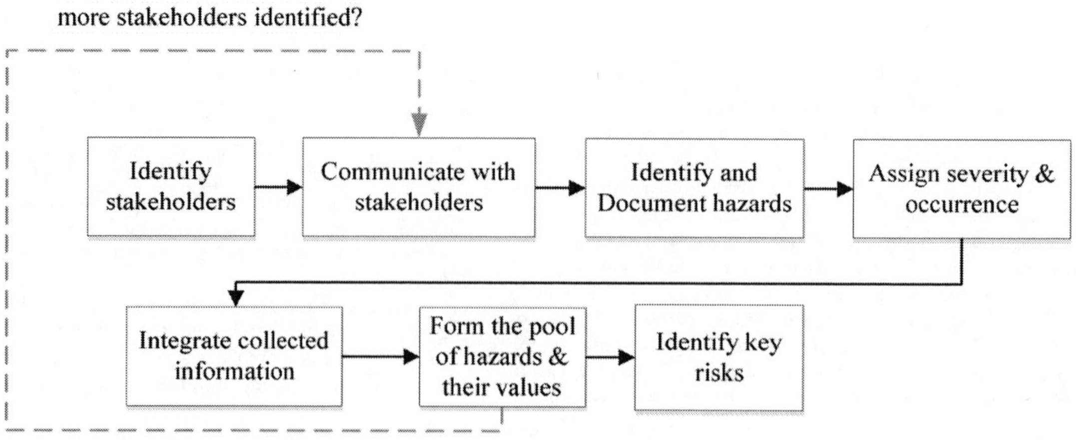

Figure 3. The process of identification of system stakeholders and system hazards.

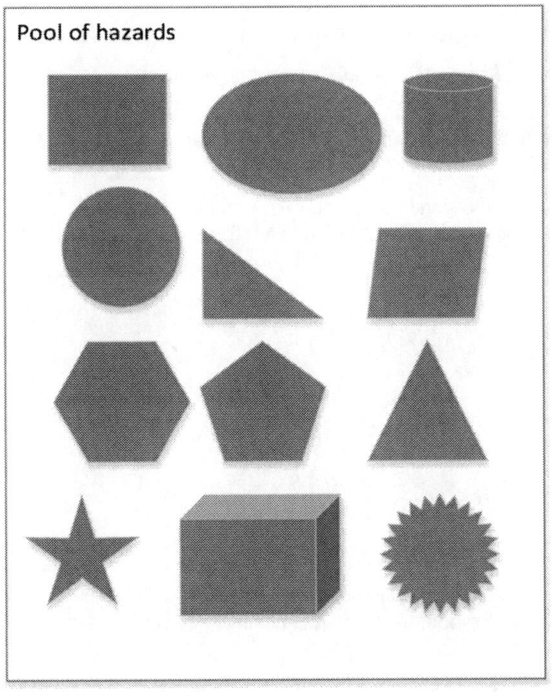

Figure 4. A schematic view for the pool of hazards. Every shape in this pool stands for a hazard.

1) *Severity of harm*

Harm is defined as physical injury or damage to persons, property, and livestock [23]. A Systems Engineer or designer is advised to define the severity of harm and communicate it with the stakeholders. For example, IEC (see [23]) defines three categories for severity of harms. This reference defines three categories of harm which are slight, high and serious as explained below.

- Slight harm which is normally reversible or reparable in short term
- High harm which is normally reversible or reparable in longer term
- Serious harm which is normally irreversible and irreparable or death.

The issue with this approach is that the user has to choose one single category, and different harms inside one category do not make differences. To overcome this and provide freedom to the user, these categories are presented in the following table and communicated with the system stakeholders. This enables the stakeholders to freely present their opinion and include their lack of certainties.

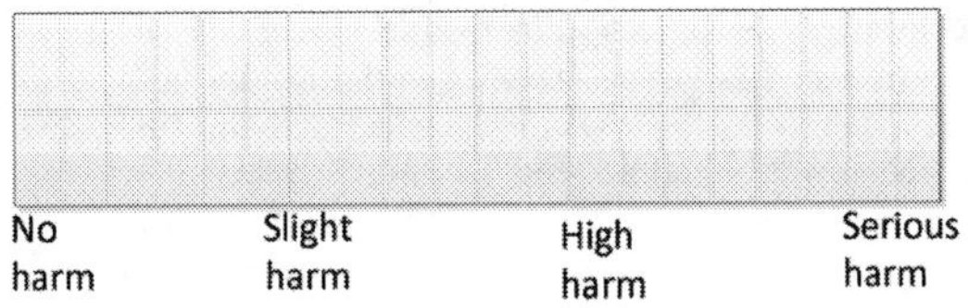

Figure 5. An example table for different categories of harm.

2) *Frequency of occurrence*

Likewise, there is a need for a standard table for communication of the frequency of occurrence for each hazard. Figure 6 presents an example table for this purpose. This table is based on the advice of [23] which suggests considering the occurrence or exposure time as a criterion for this estimation.

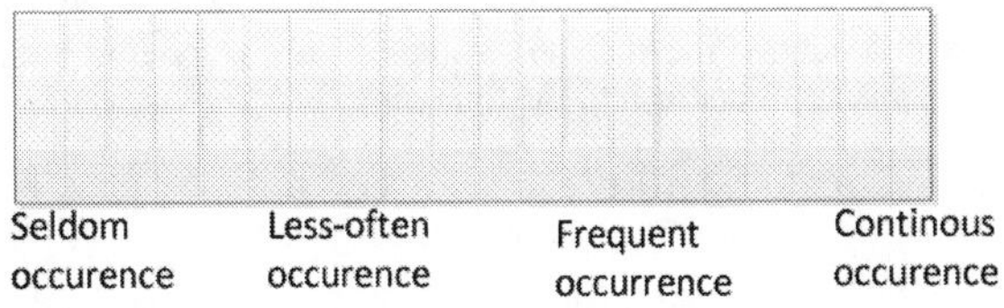

Figure 6. An example table for different frequency of occurrence.

II. METRICS FOR RISKS AND HAZARDS

In order to facilitate communication with system stakeholders, it is important to note that system has stakeholders who can be individuals, corporations, organizations and authorities, with different fields/ levels of knowledge and experience [5]. They all have their interests and expectations. Their interest may overlap, interfere or compete. This paper uses uncertainty to embed flexibility and allow a human solution in terms of preferred alternatives [24, 25]. This uncertainty is of human nature described elsewhere e.g. in [26], and its formulation will be discussed in further details through next section.

A. *Formulation of system hazard*

Having m stakeholders for a system, their opinions for the i-th hazard H_i is presented by stochastic variables $h_{i_1}, h_{i_2}, \ldots, h_{i_m}$, where h_{i_k} presents the k-th stakeholder's opinion over the importance of the i-th hazard. To analyze and rank system hazards according to expert opinion, two measures of severity and occurrence are needed for each hazard. These are further explained in the next sections.

1) *Measure of severity*

Let S_i presents the severity of H_i and let variables $s_{i_1}, s_{i_2}, \ldots, s_{i_m}$ present severity of the hazard identified by system stakeholders. The mean and standard deviation of these variables are respectively shown as $\mu^s_{i_1}, \mu^s_{i_2}, \ldots, \mu^s_{i_m}$ and $\sigma^s_{i_1}, \sigma^s_{i_2}, \ldots, \sigma^s_{i_m}$. As a result, the overall mean and standard deviation of severity of the i-th hazard are formulated by Equations (1) and (2), respectively.

$$\mu_i^s = \frac{1}{\sum_{k=1}^{m}\alpha_k}\sum_{k=1}^{m}\alpha_k\mu_{i_k}^s \quad (1)$$

$$\left(\sigma_i^s\right)^2 = \sum_{j=k}^{m}\frac{\alpha_k^2\left(\sigma_{i_k}^s\right)^2}{\left(\sum_{k=1}^{m}\alpha_k\right)^2} \quad (2)$$

Where α_k represents the assigned weight to the k-th stakeholder. If the stakeholders are evenly graded, Equations (1) and (2) transform to the following.

$$\mu_i^s = \frac{1}{m}\sum_{k=1}^{m}\mu_{i_k}^s \quad (3)$$

$$\left(\sigma_i^s\right)^2 = \sum_{k=1}^{m}\frac{\left(\sigma_{i_k}^s\right)^2}{m^2} \quad (4)$$

After normalization, the following equations are concluded.

$$\lambda_i^s = \frac{\mu_i^s}{\sum_{i=1}^{n}\mu_i^s} \quad (5)$$

$$\left(\sigma_{\lambda_i}^s\right)^2 = \left[\frac{\sigma_i^s}{\sum_{i=1}^{n}\mu_i^s}\right]^2 \quad (6)$$

Where λ_i^s and $\sigma_{\lambda_i}^s$ are respectively the weight factor and standard deviation for the i-th severity. Relative weight λ_i^s is often used as the criteria for ranking parameters. Under uncertain situation, however, λ_i^s is not the only parameter to rank severity, and its uncertainty $\sigma_{\lambda_i}^s$ can play an important role in the ranking process. High uncertainty can lead to high risk, and generally certain values are more reliable. On the basis of discussion above, we use "the reliability index for severity" as an estimated measure for the reliability of estimated severity. Therefore, the reliability index of each severity is estimated as

$$\beta_i^s = \frac{\lambda_i^s}{\sigma_{\lambda_i}^s} \quad (7)$$

The equation above indicates the relative standard error (RSE) for the estimated severity of the i-th hazard [27].

2) *Measure of occurence*

Let O_i presents the frequency of occurrence of the harm for H_i and let variables $o_{i_1}, o_{i_2}, \ldots, o_{i_m}$ present occurrence of the hazard identified by system stakeholders. The mean and standard deviation of these variables are respectively shown $\mu_{i_1}^o, \mu_{i_2}^o, \ldots, \mu_{i_m}^o$ and $\sigma_{i_1}^o, \sigma_{i_2}^o, \ldots, \sigma_{i_m}^o$. As a result, the overall mean and standard deviation of severity of the i-th hazard are formulated by Equations (1) and (2), respectively.

$$\mu_i^o = \frac{1}{\sum_{k=1}^{m}\alpha_k}\sum_{k=1}^{m}\alpha_k\mu_{i_k}^o \quad (8)$$

$$\left(\sigma_i^o\right)^2 = \sum_{j=k}^{m}\frac{\alpha_k^2\left(\sigma_{i_k}^o\right)^2}{\left(\sum_{k=1}^{m}\alpha_k\right)^2} \quad (9)$$

Where α_k represents the assigned weight to the k-th stakeholder. After normalization, the following e After normalization, the following equations are concluded.

$$\lambda_i^o = \frac{\mu_i^o}{\sum_{i=1}^{n}\mu_i^o} \quad (10)$$

$$\left(\sigma_{\lambda_i}^o\right)^2 = \left[\frac{\sigma_i^o}{\sum_{i=1}^{n}\mu_i^o}\right]^2 \quad (11)$$

Where λ_i^o and $\sigma_{\lambda_i}^o$ are respectively the weight factor and standard deviation for occurrence of i-th hazard. The reliability index for the frequency of occurrence is estimated by

$$\beta_i^o = \frac{\lambda_i^o}{\sigma_{\lambda_i}^o} \quad (12)$$

The equation above indicates the relative standard error (RSE) for the estimated occurrence of i-th hazard, which also can be referred to as reliability of the i-th occurrence [27]. It represents the degree of stakeholders' consensus.

3) *Measure of risk*

Risk is a function of severity of harm and frequency of its occurrence. In a two dimensional space of severity and occurrence, a larger distance from the origin means a larger risk. Therefore, the risk measure depends on both severity and occurrence, and it is obtained by the following formula

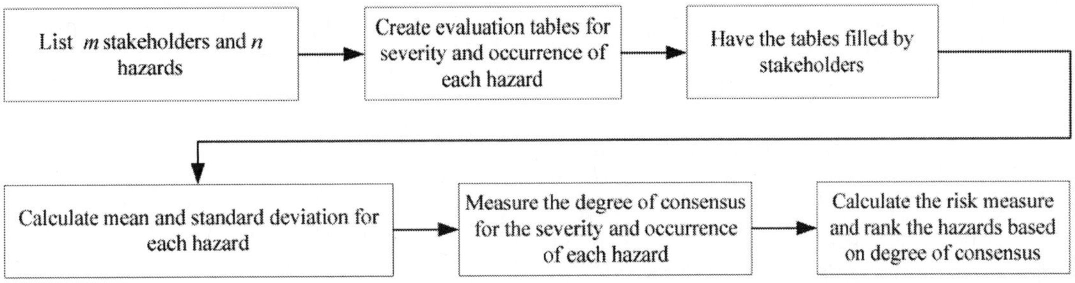

Figure 7. The process for ranking hazards.

$$R_i = \sqrt{(\beta_i^s)^2 + (\beta_i^o)^2} = \sqrt{\left(\frac{\lambda_i^s}{\sigma_{\lambda_i}^s}\right)^2 + \left(\frac{\lambda_i^o}{\sigma_{\lambda_i}^o}\right)^2} \quad (13)$$

The algorithm for applying this method is described next in Section B and an example application is presented in Section III.

B. *Algorithm*

This section describes the steps needed for ranking the risks. A summary of these steps is shown in Figure 7.

1. List m stakeholders and n concerns for system of interest. Determine the weight of stakeholders' opinions if they are not evenly graded.
2. List the hazards and make tables for their severity using the numeric or verbal format shown in Figure 5 and Figure 6.
3. Ask the stakeholders to fill the tables. This step concludes m series of tables. Use s_{i_k} format to label the collected information for each table, where k refers to the kth stakeholders.
4. Calculate the expected value and standard deviation for each table: $\mu_{i_k}^s$ and $\sigma_{i_k}^s$ for each s_{i_k}.
5. Calculate the mean and standard deviation for the severity of each hazard μ_i^s and σ_i^s.
6. Normalize the severity of hazards and calculate the relative weight factor and its uncertainty.
7. Repeat steps 2 to 6 for the frequency of occurrence instead of the severity of hazard.
8. Use Equation 13 and estimate the risk.
9. Rank the hazards based on their risk, severity, or probability of occurrence.

This process uses the collected information and sorts the system concerns based on the stakeholders' opinion. The next section presents an example application for this.

III. EXAMPLE APPLICATION

To illustrate the application of the proposed method, a simple example is presented in this section. In the example, there are four items in the pool of hazards. These hazards have been schematically shown by geometrical shapes as shown in Figure 8. This figure presents that two stakeholders have estimated the severity and frequency of occurrence of the hazards. Figure 8 (a) and (c) respectively show opinion of the first stakeholder over the severity and occurrence of the hazards. Figure 8 (b) and (d) present the opinion of the second stakeholder. The verbal explanation of the tables is not included in this example and only the numerical scale is presented. In this example, the stakeholders are not evenly graded. The importance of stakeholder 1 and stakeholder 2 are weighted as 0.7 and 0.3, respectively.

IV. DISCUSSION

Applying the algorithm explained in Section II.B results in the outcome shown in TABLE I. The first two columns of this table shows the hazards information. Columns 3 and 4 present the average of expert opinions over the severity and occurrence of harms associated to the hazards. Based on the uncertainty of these estimates, the degree of consensus is shown in Columns 5 and 6. A higher value in these columns represents a higher consensus on the stakeholder's agreement. Based on these, the risk metric is presented in the last column representing the stakeholders consensus on the values of risk. The conclusion may be drown from the risk values is that the second hazard is less risky than the others according to the stakeholder's opinion. As seen in this table, the hazards can be ranked based on the severity of harm or its frequency of occurrence. For illustration,

Figure 9 shows the risk area depicted in a two-dimensional space of severity and occurrence. Such a figure can summarize the information collected from the stakeholders and provide further insight about the risk priorities in early system design.

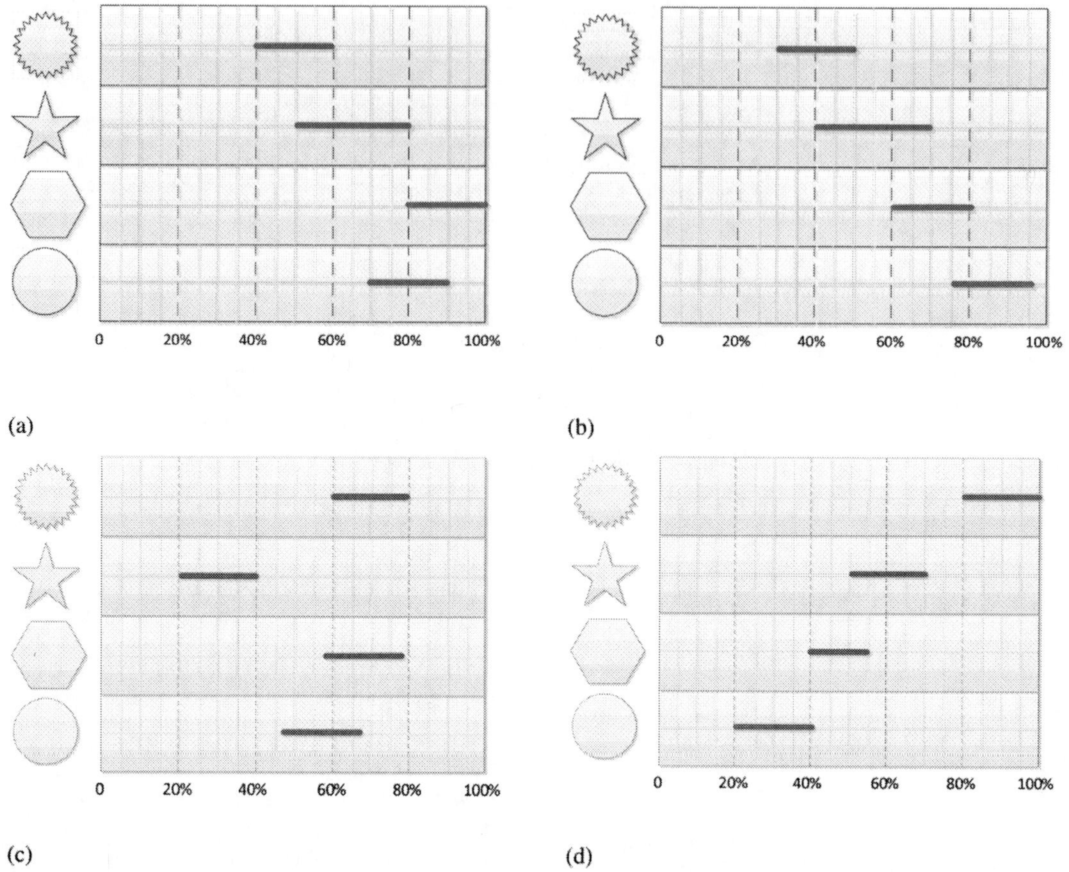

Figure 8. Figures schematically present system hazards. (a) Expert 1 presents his opinion over the severity of hazards. (b) Expert 2 presents her opinion over the severity of hazards. (c) Expert 1 presents his opinion over the frequency of occurrence of hazards. (d) Expert 2 presents her opinion over the frequency of occurrence of hazards.

This example shows how the method is used to communicate with stakeholders, register their concerns, integrate the collected data and disclose the most important aspects. Similar results have been achieved through real-world case studies to prioritize the stakeholder consensus in terms of project requirements. See for example [26, 28].

TABLE 1. THIS TABLE PRESENTS THE REQUIREMENTS AND THEIR WEIGHT FACTORS, STANDARD DEVIATIONS, RELATIVE WEIGHTS, UNCERTAINTIES IN RELATIVE WEIGHT, RELATIVE UNCERTAINTIES AND DEGREE OF CONSENSUS.

ID	Hazards	Expected severity (μ_i^s %)	Expected occurrence (μ_i^o %)	Consensus over severity β_i^s	Consensus over occurrence β_i^o	Estimated Risk (R_i %)
HZ1	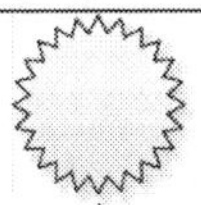	40	90	3,1	6,7	10
HZ2		55	60	2,8	3,8	6
HZ3	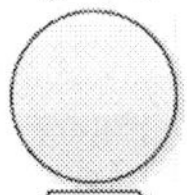	70	48	5,6	5,5	11
HZ4	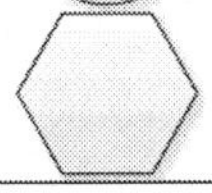	88	30	5,9	3,6	10

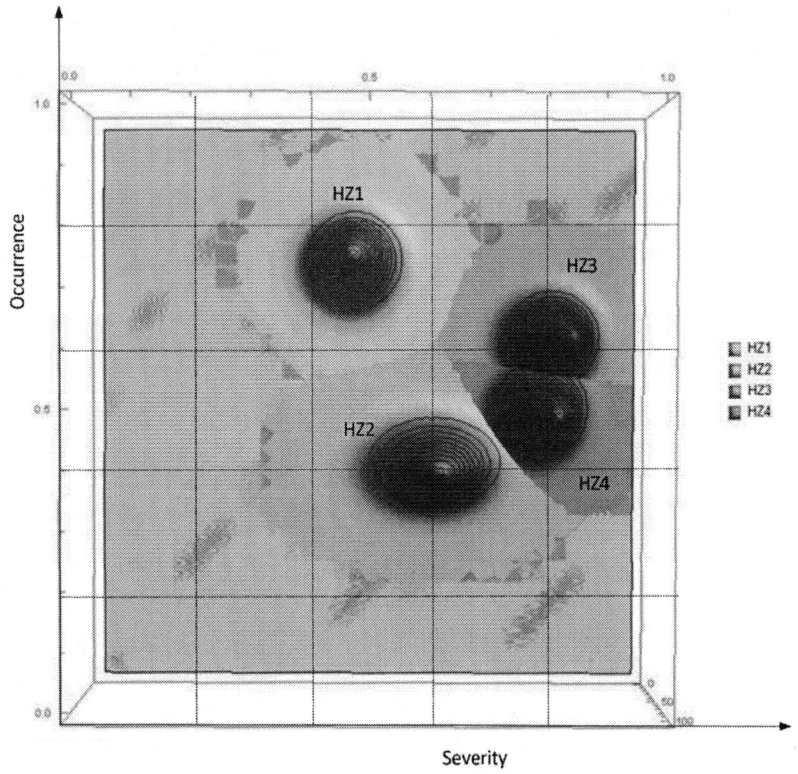

Figure 9. Two-dimensional representation of risks. Risks are presented in this picture through two categories of severity of harm and its occurrence.

V. Conclusions

The paper proposes a graphical tool to communicate with stakeholders, collect the risk information and combine it in order to prioritize the system risks. A pluralistic approach is used to probabilistically measure the severity of harm and frequency of occurrence. These metrics are used to find the degree of stakeholders' consensus over system risks and rank them. The proposed approach is based on probability theory and promotes probabilistic thinking. The use of this outcome for triangulation of risk concerns is the next step for this research.

Rferences

1. Rajabalinejad, M., *Coping with System Hazards in Early Project Life Cycle: Identification and Prioritization*, in *The Sixth International Conference on Performance, Safety and Robustness in Complex Systems and Applications*. 2016: Lisbon, Portugal.
2. Beck, G. and C. Kropp, *Infrastructures of risk: a mapping approach towards controversies on risks.* Journal of risk research, 2011. **14**(1): p. 1-16.
3. ISO, *ISO 12100:2010 Safety of machinery - General principles for design - Risk assessment and risk reduction*. 2010.
4. Standard, B., *BS EN 31010:2010 Risk management - Risk assessment techniques*. 2010.
5. Rajabalinejad, M. and C. Spitas, *Incorporating Uncertainty into the Design Management Process.* Design Management Journal, 2012. **6**(1): p. 52-67.
6. ISO, *ISO 31000:2009 Risk management — Principles and guidelines*. 2009.
7. Engel, A. and T.R. Browning, *Designing systems for adaptability by means of architecture options.* Systems Engineering, 2008. **11**(2): p. 125-146.
8. Leveson, N., *Engineering a Safer World.* 2012, Cambridge, Massachusetts, London, England: Massachusetts Institute of Technology.
9. Rajabalinejad, M., G.M. Bonnema, and F.J.A.M.v. Houten, *An integral safety approach for design of high risk products and systems*, in *Safety and Reliability of Complex Engineered Systems* P.e. al., Editor. 2015, Taylor & Francis Group: Zurich, Switzerland.
10. Christel, M.G. and K.C. Kang, *Issues in requirements elicitation*. 1992, DTIC Document.
11. Heemels, W., et al., *The key driver method.* Boderc: Model-Based Design of High-Tech Systems, edited by W. Heemels and GJ Muller, 2006: p. 27-42.
12. Heemels, W., E. vd Waal, and G. Muller, *A multi-disciplinary and model-based design methodology for high-tech systems.* Proceedings of CSER, 2006.
13. Pahl, G., W. Beitz, and K. Wallace, *Engineering design: a systematic approach*. 1996: Springer Verlag.
14. Whitten, J.L., V.M. Barlow, and L. Bentley, *Systems analysis and design methods*. 1997: McGraw-Hill Professional.
15. Barron, F.H. and B.E. Barrett, *Decision quality using ranked attribute weights.* Management Science, 1996. **42**(11): p. 1515-1523.
16. Takeda, E., K.O. Cogger, and P.L. Yu, *Estimating criterion weights using eigenvectors: A comparative study.* European Journal of Operational Research, 1987. **29**(3): p. 360-369.
17. Saaty, T.L. and L.G. Vargas, *The logic of priorities: applications in business, energy, health, and transportation*. 1982: Kluwer-Nijhoff.
18. Barzilai, J., *Deriving weights from pairwise comparison matrices.* Journal of the Operational Research Society, 1997. **48**(12): p. 1226-1232.
19. Yeh, C.-H., et al., *Task oriented weighting in multi-criteria analysis.* European Journal of Operational Research, 1999. **119**(1): p. 130-146.
20. Buckley, J.J., *Ranking alternatives using fuzzy numbers.* Fuzzy Sets and Systems, 1985. **15**(1): p. 21-31.
21. Tsai, W.C., *A Fuzzy Ranking Approach to Performance eEaluation of Quality*. 2011. Vol. 18. 2011.
22. Mitchell, H.B., *Rnking-Intuitionistic Fuzzy Numbers.* International Journal of Uncertainty, Fuzziness and Knowledge-Based Systems, 2004. **12**(03): p. 377-386.
23. Commision, I.E., *IEC GUIDE 116 Edition 1.0 2010-08 Guidelines for safety related risk assessment and risk reduction for low voltage equipment.*
24. Zimmermann, H.J., *Fuzzy sets, decision making and expert systems*. Vol. 10. 1987: Springer.
25. Rajabalinejad, M. *Modelling dependencies and couplings in the design space of meshing gear sets.* 2012.
26. Rajabalinejad, M. and G.M. Bonnema, *Probabilistic thinking to support early evaluation of system quality: through requirement analysis*, in *5th International Conference on Complex Systems Design & Management (CSD&M) 2014, Paris, 12-14 November*. 2014: Paris.
27. Melchers, R.E., *Structural reliability analysis and prediction.* 1999.
28. Rajabalinejad, M. and G.M. Bonnema. *Determination of stakeholders' consensus over values of system of systems.* in *Proceedings of the 9th International Conference on System of Systems Engineering: The Socio-Technical Perspective, SoSE 2014*. 2014.

Citizens Broadband Radio Service Spectrum Sharing Framework - A New Strategic Option for Mobile Network Operators?

Seppo Yrjölä
Nokia
Oulu, Finland
email: seppo.yrjola@nokia.com

Abstract **- The paper seeks to identify mobile network operators' business opportunities and strategic options in the new Citizens Broadband Radio Service shared spectrum access framework. More flexible and scalable utilization of the 3.5 GHz spectrum aims to increase the efficiency of spectrum use in delivering fast growing and converging mobile broadband and media services while paving way to new innovations, e.g., in the area of Internet of Things and 5th Generation. The opportunity analysis and created simple strategic rules indicated that the mobile network operators could benefit significantly from the new, shared Citizens Broadband Radio Service bands enabling them to cope with increasing asymmetric media data traffic, and to offer differentiation through improved quality and personalization of services. Furthermore, through unbundling investment in spectrum, network infrastructure and services co-operative business opportunities may open with vertical segments, new alternative operator types and the Internet domain. The concepts of co-opetition and simple rules strategic framework were found useful to characterize the business environment regarding spectrum sharing. Heterogeneous network assets leveraging the Third Generation Partnership Program's Long Term Evolution were found to be the key enabler while regulatory actions may frame the availability of spectrum and limit the economic value for an operator.**

Keywords - business model; Citizens Broadband Radio Service; mobile broadband; spectrum sharing; strategy.

I. INTRODUCTION

We have witnessed the rapid growth of wireless services with a large range of diverse devices, applications and services requiring connectivity. The number of mobile broadband (MBB) data subscribers, connected 'things' and the amount of data used per user is set to grow significantly leading to increasing spectrum demand, and need for novel spectrum management techniques, and related new business models discussed in the COCORA 2016 [1]. The US President's Council of Advanced Science & Technology (PCAST) report [2] emphasized the need for novel thinking within wireless industry to meet the growing spectrum needs [3], and to tackle crisis in spectrum allocation, utilization and management. The essential role of spectrum sharing and dynamic spectrum access were underlined to find a balance between the different systems and services with their different spectrum requirements and system dynamics. For any spectrum-sharing framework, where several radio systems operate in the same spectrum to be a feasible and attractive, early cooperation across regulation, business and technology domains is essential. Collaboration in the technology and innovation domain between industry and research enables validation of the enabling technologies and new concepts while ensuring economies of scale and scope in implementation. Furthermore, regulation has a key enabler role through spectrum harmonization and providing incentives for early adopter while on the other hand, defines limiting factors and competition framework. The spectrum regulation has played central role in the wireless ecosystems in creating current multibillion business ecosystems, for MBB operator businesses via exclusive Quality of Service (QoS) spectrum usage rights, and at the same time for unlicensed wireless local area network (Wi-Fi) ecosystem drawing from the public spurring innovations.

So far, only a subset of the spectrum sharing research has reached the regulation domain, the early studies on cognitive radio (CR) on license exempt access with intelligent user terminals and spectrum sensing as the general interference mitigation technique as one example. Furthermore, several spectrum sharing concepts widely studied, standardized and supported by national regulatory authorities (NRA) has not scaled up commercially as expected, TV White Space (TVWS) [4][5] being the latest example. Based on the decade of profound CR, and in particular unlicensed TVWS concept studies, a couple of novel licensing based sharing models have recently emerged and are under regulatory discussion and early stage standardization, the Licensed Shared Access (LSA) [6] from Europe and the Citizens Broadband Radio Service (CBRS) from the US [7]. This paper investigates:

1) How can the CBRS spectrum sharing be defined for Mobile Network Operators (MNOs)?
2) What are MNOs' business opportunities, and how are they framed regarding the CBRS?
3) What kind of strategic choices do MNOs have to make regarding spectrum sharing?

The rest of the paper is organized as follows. First, the state of art and the research gap is shortly discussed in Section II. Second, the CBRS 3-tier sharing framework is presented and defined for a MNO in Section III. Theoretical background for co-opetitive business opportunity framework and the Simple Rules strategic approach is introduced in Section IV. The elements framing business opportunities and

Simple Rules strategic options are derived and evaluated in Section V. Finally, conclusions are drawn in Section VI.

II. STATE OF THE ART

For the prominent spectrum-sharing concepts currently under research, particularly the CBRS, there is not much prior work available regarding their business model or strategic analysis. An initial evaluation of the general spectrum-sharing concept from the business modeling point of view can be found in [8] and the LSA focused analysis from [9][10]. The feasibility and attractiveness of the LSA and the CBRS spectrum sharing concepts were analyzed in [11]. Furthermore, key stakeholders' capability to deal with combined internal and external resources and capabilities in doing business utilizing the CBRS concept was analyzed in [12] based on the Dynamic Capability strategic management framework. That work is extended by focusing on the dynamic CBRS sharing concept, and analyzing the MNO business opportunities using the co-opetitive (co-operation and competition) business opportunity framework and the Simple Rules strategic framework [13].

III. CITIZENS BROADBAND RADIO SERVICE SPECTRUM SHARING FRAMEWORK

The key policy messages of the PCAST report were further strengthened in 2013 with the Presidential Memorandum [14] stating "*...we must make available even more spectrum and create new avenues for wireless innovation. One means of doing so is by allowing and encouraging shared access to spectrum that is currently allocated exclusively for Federal use. Where technically and economically feasible, sharing can and should be used to enhance efficiency among all users and expedite commercial access to additional spectrum bands, subject to adequate interference protection for Federal users, we should also seek to eliminate restrictions on commercial carriers' ability to negotiate sharing arrangements with agencies. To further these efforts, while still safeguarding protected incumbent systems that are vital to Federal interests and economic growth, this memorandum directs agencies and offices to take a number of additional actions to accelerate shared access to spectrum.*"

Followed by intense discussion and consultation with the industry the Federal Communications Commission (FCC) released Report and Order and Second Further Notice of Proposed Rulemaking to establish new rules for shared use of the 3550-3650 MHz band in April 2015 [7]. The FCC sees the opening of the 3.5 GHz Band as "*a new chapter in the history of the administration of one of our nation's most precious resources—the electromagnetic radio spectrum.*" The framework defines a contiguous 150 MHz block at 3550-3700 MHz for MBB that the FCC calls Citizens Broadband Radio Service. The 3550-3650 MHz spectrum is currently allocated for use by the US Department of Defense (DoD) radar systems and Fixed Satellite Services (FSS), while the 3650-3700 MHz spectrum incumbents are the FSS and the grandfathered commercial wireless broadband services.

The FCC prefigures CBRS as an "*innovation band*", where they can assign spectrum to commercial MBB systems like the 3rd Generation Partnership Program (3GPP) Long Term Evolution (LTE) on a shared basis with incumbent radar and FSS systems and promote a diversity of Heterogonous Network (HetNet) technologies, particularly small cells. The sharing framework consists of three tiers: *Incumbent Access* (IA), *Priority Access* (PA) and *General Authorized Access* (GAA), as shown in the Fig. 1.

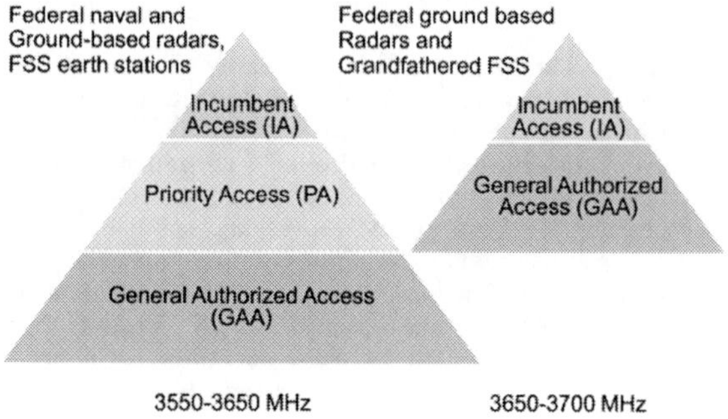

Figure 1. The US CBRS 3-tiered authorization framework with the FCC's spectrum access models for 3550-3650MHz and 3650-3700MHz spectrum segments.

The PA users will obtain a FCC PA license (PAL) to operate up to 70 MHz of the 3550-3650 MHz spectrum segment, and are protected from harmful interference from the GAA operations. The PA layer covers critical access users like hospitals, utilities and governmental users and non-critical users, e.g., MNOs. PA users receive short term priority authorization to operate within designated geographic areas with the PALs such as 3 year 10 MHz unpaired channel in a single census track, awarded with competitive bidding. During the first application window only, an applicant may apply for up to two consecutive three-year terms for any given PAL. Licenses will be permitted to hold no more than four PALs in one census tract at one time. This will ensure the availability of PAL spectrum to at least two licensed users in the geographic areas of highest demand. PALs are assigned specific frequencies within their service area, and at the end of its term, a PAL will automatically terminate, and may not be renewed.

The third GAA tier will operate under a *licensed-by-rule* framework and will be allowed throughout the 150 MHz band without any interference protection from other CBRS users. This framework aims to facilitate the rapid deployment of compliant small cell devices, while minimizing administrative costs and burdens on the public, licensees, and the FCC. GAA users may use only certified, the FCC approved CBRS devices, and must register with a SAS with information required by the rules, e.g., operator identity (ID), device identification, and geo-location information.

In the CBRS functional architecture [15] depicted in the Fig. 2, *CBRS Devices* (CBSDs), which are fixed stations, or networks of such stations will be assigned spectrum dynamically by the FCC selected SAS, which could be multiple. In case of a CBSD is a managed network as in the typical case of MNOs, CBSD network includes a *domain proxy (DP)* and a network management functionality as shown in the Fig. 3. A DP's function is to accept a set of one or more available channels and select channels for use by specific CBSDs, or alternatively pass the available channels to the operators Operation Administration and Maintenance (OAM) Network Management System (NMS) for CBSD channel selection. In practical implementation, OAM NMS may be co-located with the DP. The DP back reports selected channels to a SAS optionally received via a NMS, and receives confirmation of channel assignment from a SAS.

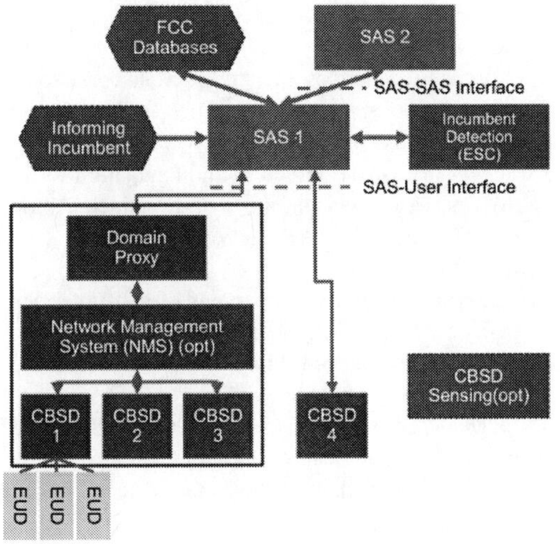

Figure 2. The CBRS functional architecture.

Furthermore, the DP performs bidirectional bulk CBSD registration and directive processing through operator NMS if present. Additional bidirectional information processing and routing function may include, e.g., interference reporting.

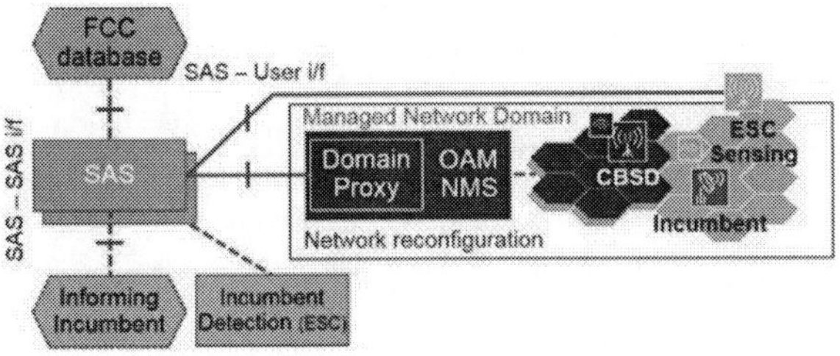

Figure 3. The Domain Proxy in the CBRS functional architecture.

To summarize, the DP could be a pure bidirectional information processing and routing engine, or a more intelligent mediation function, e.g., combining the small cells of a mall or a sports arena to a virtual CBSD entity that covers the complete mall or sports arena. The latter option allows flexible self-control and interference optimizations in such a network. End user devices (EUD), e.g., handsets are not considered as CBSDs.

The SAS controls the interference environment and enforces exclusion zones to protect higher priority users, as well as takes care of registration, authentication and identification of user information. As the IA users have primary spectrum rights at all times and in all areas over PA and GAA, all the CBRS users must be capable of operating across the entire 3.5 GHz band, and discontinuing operation or changing frequencies at the direction of the SAS to protect the IA. Automated channel assignment by a SAS will simply involve instructions to these users to use a specific channel, at a specific place and time, within 3550-3700MHz. The SAS would obtain the FCC information, e.g., about registered or licensed commercial users, exclusion zone areas requiring sensing from the FCC database. *Informing incumbent* architecture option allows the federal IA to inform the SAS ahead of plans to use the spectrum in some area, e.g., related to planed use of the spectrum. The SAS could be administrated by a third party or a mobile operator as an *operator SAS*. By operating own operator SAS, MNOs may better control their business operation critical information flow and sharing between their MBB network and the third party administrated SAS. However, all the SAS systems should be FCC certified and meet all the SAS requirements set forth by the FCC and the WINN Forum specifications.

It will be mandatory for all the CBRS users to protect the IA users in the band. Based on nature and critical requirements of the federal incumbent the FCC adopted rules to require *Environmental Sensing Capabilities* (ESCs) to detect federal spectrum use in and adjacent to the 3.5 GHz the band. The federal IA user protection will be adopted in two phases. In the first phase, a large portion of the country outside the static exclusion zones will be available after SAS is commercially available and FCC approved. At the second phase, the rest of the country, including major coastal areas, will become available as exclusion zones will be converted to protection zones through the ESC system detecting federal incumbent use. The SAS receives input from ESCs, and if needed, could order commercial tier users to vacate a spectrum resource in frequency, location, or time, which when in proximity to federal incumbent presents a risk of harmful interference.

Prospective ESC operators must have their systems approved through the same process for SASs and SAS administrators. An ESC consists of one or more commercially operated networks of device-based or infrastructure-based sensors that would be used to detect signals from federal radar systems in the vicinity of the exclusion zones. Within 300 seconds after the ESC communication of a detected federal system signal, the SAS must confirm either suspension or relocation of operations to another unoccupied frequency.

The opportunistic GAA with no interference protection from other CBRS users is planned to provide a low-cost entry point into the CBRS band for a wide array of users and services first while PAL system operations have to wait auction process estimated to start after the US 600 MHz incentive auctions in 2016 -2017. For the meanwhile, the FCC has encouraged multi-stakeholder groups to consider various issues raised by the rules. The Wireless Innovation Forum (WINNF) Spectrum Sharing Committee (SSC) [16] with representatives from the MBB, Wireless broadband, Internet, Internet of Things (IoT) / machine to machine (m2m) and defense ecosystems has started standardization work on interfaces between a MBB system and a SAS work targeted to allow sharing of the CBRS till end of the year 2016.

The US Government has initially identified an additional 2 GHz of spectrum below 6 GHz owned by the DoD and other users for future shared commercial use conditionally if the spectrum sharing at 3.5 GHz proves successful. This paves way to make licensed spectrum sharing a third mainstream way of licensing spectrum to commercial users complementing traditional exclusive licensing and unlicensed spectrum access. The FCC has vision to repeat Wi-Fi success through lowering the entry barrier QoS spectrum for new entrants and verticals, e.g., enterprise, utilities, healthcare, public safety, smart cities, etc.

IV. Business Opportunity Based Simple Rules Strategic Framework

In this section, we introduce business and strategy frameworks used in analyzing the business opportunities and strategic options for a MNO utilizing CBRS spectrum.

A. Co-opetitive Business Opportuntiy Framework

An entrepreneurial opportunity can be defined as the possibility to serve customers better and differently [17] framed by enablers, limiting factors, and challenges caused by the business context. Fig. 4 below depicts the framework used in this paper to develop and frame the business opportunities for MNOs.

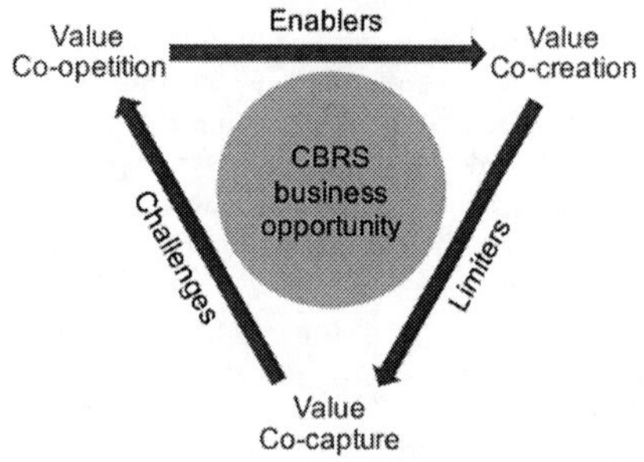

Figure 4. The Co-opetitive business opportunity framework.

In the CBRS context, business opportunities are made to create and deliver value for the stakeholders, value that is co-created among various actors from MBB, wireless and incumbent ecosystems as a joint effort. An equally important aspect is the ability of the stakeholders to capture value, i.e., obtain profits [18], which in the context of this study can be called value co-capture. Furthermore, value co-creation can be seen as a cooperative and the parallel value co-capture as a competitive process [19]. The third term co-opetition illustrates the increased system complexity of the CBRS business environment, where companies simultaneously compete and cooperate with each other not only over spectrum resources but also over customers.

B. Business Model Typology

A coherent 4C typology was created to classify Internet era business models, and to make the business model analysis easier and more structured [20]. The typology introduces four prototypical models, each with varying value propositions and revenue models [20]:

1) *Commerce* enables low transaction costs for buyers and sellers of goods and services; Direct sales revenues and indirect streams as commissions,

2) *Context* provides structure and navigation for Internet user to increase transparency and reduce complexity typically based on transaction independent online advertisement revenues,

3) *Content* delivers various types of consumer centered, personalized content; Mainly indirect revenue streams like online advertisement, premium content increasingly with subscription or usage pricing, and

4) *Connection* provides network infrastructure and related services that enable exchange of information and users' participation having both the direct and indirect revenue stream models.

Different stakeholders of the ecosystem can implement these business models alone or combined as a hybrid, which is an important aspect in relation to sharing. The business potential of the whole ecosystem depends on the ecosystem players' synergies when providing their services. Furthermore, the 4C typology can be interpreted as "layers" where a "lower" layer business models are required as enabler and value levers for higher layers to exist as depicted in Fig. 5 in the analysis Section V.

C. Simple Rules Strategic Framework

Business literature provides us with numerous examples of business strategy approaches and strategic elements applied. Traditional strategic logic based on position focuses on answering the question: *where* should we be through identifying an attractive market segment and sustainable position and then establishing, strengthening and defending it, e.g., [21]. In structured businesses, another widely used approach is built around leveraging core competences and resources, i.e., *What* to achieve sustained long-term market dominance, e.g., [22].

In rapidly changing complex markets, like today's wireless communications, traditional approaches have faced several limitations: they do not build around the business opportunity, have only weak linkages to the key business processes, depict resources rather than activities, and lack needed flexibility to seize fast changing opportunities. In this paper, the strategic *Simple Rules* approach presented in [13] was adopted, that partly helps to answer to the concerns discussed above.

In emerging and dynamic business environments, the novel Simple Rules approach sees business strategies as built around the opportunity and the key processes needed to seize them flexibly and timely. The strategic approach provides practical guidelines within, which opportunities could be pursued with selected key processes. The proposed framework consists of five categories:

1) *How-to* rules for conducting business in an unique, differentiating way,
2) *Boundary* rules for defining the boundaries of the business opportunities of the stakeholders,
3) *Priority* rules that help to identify and rank the criteria for opportunity decision making,
4) *Timing* rules that help in synchronizing, coordinating and pacing emerging opportunities, and
5) *Exit* rules that help in identifying basis for exit or selecting initiatives to be stopped.

V. Analysis of the Strategic Opportunities

The business opportunities and strategic choices as Simple Rules created and their analysis are summarized in this section.

A. Elements Framing Business Opportunities

In the analysis for the business opportunity elements of the CBRS, five key ecosystem roles were identified: the NRA, federal incumbent, MNOs, SAS administrator, infrastructure vendors and device/chip manufactures. In the systemic framework change like the CBRS, all the stakeholders play a vital role in adopting of the novel CBRS concept and spectrum sharing in general. In addition, when developing and analyzing the opportunity frame authors argue that three domains; regulation, business, and technology, affecting spectrum sharing concept should proceed in tandem. Enabling, limiting and challenging elements framing the business opportunities for a MNO are next discussed and summarized in Table I.

Business and technology elements can be identified as *enablers* for value co-creation. Fast growing demand and lack of exclusive spectrum combined with the drastic changes in the consumption habits will urge the adoption of novel more flexible and efficient spectrum management concepts. Framework radically unbundles investment in spectrum, network infrastructure and services, and enables novel services and business models. Furthermore, different spectrum sharing schemes are high in regulators agenda with aims to lower the entry barrier to spectrum for new alternative types of operators, which could consider entering the wireless broadband business. Utilization of the LTE ecosystem scale and harmonization will reduce risk related technology maturity, and provide tools to seamlessly integrate additional spectrum capacity to MNOs HetNet, e.g., through modern techniques like Carrier Aggregation (CA) [23], LTE Unlicensed (LTE-U/LAA) [24] or MulteFire [25], and Self Organizing Network (SON) load balancing and traffic steering [26].

Furthermore, as content is increasingly over-the-top (OTT) video and multimedia, Mobile Edge Computing (MEC) platform can rapidly process content at the very edge of the mobile network, delivering an Quality of Experience (QoE) that is ultra-responsive as latency is significantly reduced. The MEC will take a full advantage of the localized shared spectrum resources and telco cloud, enabling new possibilities to serve the operator's radio network and to co-exist with other virtualized network functions [27]. Big data analytics capabilities will play a major role in coping with the SAS dynamic requirements and enabling low transaction costs, and in the future enabling spectrum aggregator and broker models.

Regarding *limiting factors*, sound, sustainable and harmonized regulatory environment can be the limiter that needs to be addressed before a MNO can co-create and co-capture value from it with ecosystem partners. The limited spectrum availability in frequency, time or location with potential restriction and uncertainties may negatively influence MNOs outlook on shared use and the spectrum valuation. A specific technology item to be considered is the degree of business (MNOs) and mission (DoD) critical information needed to share and resulting need for the ESC system. In addition to MNO opportunities, it is essential to consider reciprocal incentives for the current federal spectrum holders to further transition to CBRS.

Policy risk and uncertainty are the main elements of the co-opetitive *challenges* in the competitive domain. MNOs traditionally used to operate with exclusive spectrum rights framework will see strategic risks with moving towards interference-protected rights only provided by the CBRS. Fragmented national and global market structure deprives economies of scale and scope, raising costs and hampering innovation in the ecosystem. Furthermore, introduction of sharing models may influence the MNOs current exclusive spectrum licensing model and it is availability in the future. The regulatory approach, and in particular the 3-tier concept could unbundle investment in spectrum, network infrastructure and services. Faster access to spectrum with lower initial investment (annuity payments for spectrum rights) enables local 'pro-competitive' deployments and further expands sharing mechanism for pooling spectrum and infra resources between operators. Furthermore, the IoT and 5G era also opens up opportunities for new competition, especially in the traffic hotspots with specific venues with very specific interest to be fulfilled, e.g., hospitals, sporting events, shopping malls, universities will attract new players.

At the same time, the complexity of the CBRS framework and the SAS might influence the value of the spectrum and the required time of recovering the network investments. On the competence domain, MNOs need to pay attention to dynamic capabilities needed to deploy, manage and optimize multilayered HetNets under sharing conditions.

TABLE I. ELEMENTS FRAMING BUSINESS OPPORTUNITIES

	Business opportunity framing elements
Enablers	• Lack of exclusive spectrum triggers new spectrum access approaches • Consumers MBB consumption habits are changing towards asymmetric multi-device usage • Shared spectrum allocation improves overall spectrum use efficiency • Regulators considering shared spectrum framework in Europe and the US • Unbundles investment in spectrum, network infrastructure and services • Additional lower cost capacity to cope with asymmetric traffic and improve performance • Better QoS spectrum may increase dense urban area business • Additional GAA capacity for offloading and local services • May lower entry barriers for challenger MNOs and new alternative type of operators • Harmonized LTE technology base leverage HetNet asset optimization and offers scale • Mobile Edge Computing improves QoS and QoE of localized services • Big data and analytics capabilities with Internet domain
Limiters	• Limited spectrum availability and predictability limit MNO business opportunities • Need for global and national regulation outside of the US may slow down entry - Harmonization is a precondition to scale and enable potential benefit fully. • Real incentives for the federal incumbents unclear or missing • Federal incumbent special requirements in particular related to security and need for sensing • Regulatory framework restrictions may reduce the economic value • Degree of information sharing of business critical (MNOs) and secret information (Federal incumbent) and needed ESC system • Standardization of SAS functionalities for 3GPP ecosystem and technologies needed
Challenges	• Uncertainty and risks related to regulation in timing, term, licenses and flexibility creates exposure and risk for a MNO to proceed with the investment. • Impact on exclusive spectrum licensing model and availability in the future • Attractive and dynamic spectrum market with potentially lower transaction costs. • May increase and change competition. New operator types, and from other business domains. • Increased technical and operational complexity (SAS) with related capital and operational costs • New competencies and capabilities needed for network management and optimization • Timely availability of full band base stations and terminals and potential impact on cost and complexity

Traditional MNOs support for the 3.5GHz spectrum in their networks is paramount to encourage chip and device manufacturers to support the whole 3.5GHz band introduction with competitive terminals. Attractive and dynamic spectrum market with potentially lower transaction costs may increase and change competition, e.g., through introducing new and alternative operator types locally and from other business domains. On the other hand, introduction alternative local operators offer co-opetitive collaboration opportunities for a MNO, e.g., through sharing infrastructure and or network capacity.

B. Business Opportunities

In this section, business opportunities are discussed based on their key framing elements from Sub-section A, and summarized utilizing the 4C business model typology.

There is a need to fundamentally design future spectrum sharing enabled and complemented networks not just to service new use-cases, but also enable new business models. The industry is moving from today's "bit pipe" connectivity business models for MBB monetizing connectivity and 3rd party content (like video) towards "smart pipes" capturing value from digital content & information from the cloud and consider offering connectivity, in some cases free-of change. This will turn mobile broadband business from competitive value creation and capture thinking toward co-opetitive sharing economy, multitude of ecosystems to work with.

In order to realize the business potential of the novel dynamically shared spectrum resources, MNOs have occasion to simultaneously co-create and co-capture value with ecosystem players in a co-opetitive business environment where co-operation (spectrum, infrastructure assets) and competition (customers & services) exist parallel to each other. MNOs are in unique position to leverage additional multi-tiered capacity the CBRS concept offers. Faster access to QoS licensed small cell optimized spectrum without mandatory coverage obligations will help them to timely cope with booming asymmetric data needs more locally when and where needed. Additional scalable and flexible spectrum resource leveraged with LTE technology enablers will enable them to better retain and grow existing customer base with changing demand and consumer habits.

MNOs business models and opportunities are powered by premium network performance, information brokering and network as a service. The premium performance level of networks enables novel broadband services such as High Definition (HD) video and Virtual Reality (VR)/Augmented Reality (AR) services in the home, on the move, and for the business world. These *Premium Connectivity* business models provide new opportunities by guaranteed high service levels not only with end users, but also with content and other service providers. As content is increasingly OTT video and multimedia, *Mobile Edge Computing* capabilities can rapidly process content at the very edge of the mobile network, delivering an experience that is highly responsive as latency is significantly reduced. Premium connectivity enables partner-based propositions and allows for faster development and launch of these partner services at the benefit of all.

The increasing number of control and transaction *data* produced by the network can be particularly leveraged in new vertical segments. The innovation possible in the IoT and 5G use cases involves bringing massive internal and external data sets together to uncover new insights to add value in new sharing economy based services. MNOs with needed big data and analytics dynamic capabilities will be optimally positioned to broker information with different business domains such as providers of augmented reality services, smart cities, factories, logistics, health, and utilities.

Dedicated virtual sub-networks, the *network slices*, can be modelled as *Network as Service (NaaS),* which provide exactly the functionality needed for different verticals and industries with their diverse use cases. E.g., use case of consumer health sensors is completely different to ultra-high quality video delivery. On-demand, as-a-service business models play essential role in the timely sharing economy concept, defined as "*the value in taking the underutilized assets and making them accessible online to a community, leading to a reduced need for ownership of those assets [28].*"

In the NaaS concept, all elements of the network from radio access, core network and Operations Support System (OSS) to security and analytics can be virtualized through Network Function Virtualization (NFV), and sliced out as one integrated service. This enables an operator to create an instance of an entire network virtually relying on whatever underlying infrastructure is available for the defined geography. With the power of programmability in the Software Defined Networking (SDN) of the networks, it should be further possible to customize such a 'network instance' for vertical *Anything-as-a-Service* (XaaS) solutions, e.g., for logistics, automotive, healthcare, utilities, or retail.

In Fig. 5, discussed business opportunities are mapped into the 4C Internet business typology. Currently, the main source of revenue for MNOs drives from subscriber retail markets based on the connectivity. Through leveraging additional flexible capacity, MNOs are in good position to expand their business model to cover wholesale, where one party gets spectrum, build, owns and operates the LTE access network and leases bandwidth to virtual operators, subject to QoS controlled by dynamic Service Level Agreements (SLAs). Utilizing discussed NFV and SDN technologies, the model could be further developed to provide connectivity as a Service to new alternative operators. Edge computing and data monetization enables MNOs to enter higher layer content and context models in collaboration with new customer from verticals and other industries with new growth opportunities.

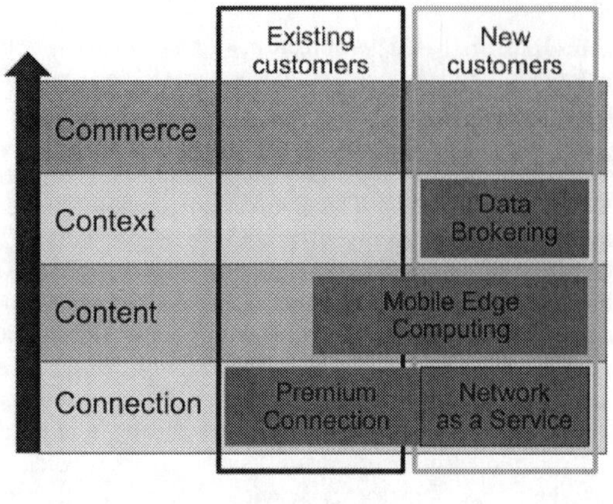

Figure 5. The MNO business opportunties mapped into 4C business model typology.

C. *Simple Rules*

In this Sub-section strategic rules applying the Simple Rules strategy approach from [13] for MNOs deploying the CBRS were created and analyzed for the business opportunities identified and discussed in the Sub-section B. Created Simple Rules are summarized in Table II.

MNOs' *How-to rules* for conducting business in a unique and differentiating way continues to be based on the dominant market position and lock-ins through Customer data and Experience Management (CEM). This could be reached by gaining access, if possible, to all available exclusive spectrum, and by combining existing and new shared CBRS spectrum assets to deliver premium connectivity service in QoS and QoE. Sharing terms and conditions, particularly at the PAL layer, such as term, predictability, certainty and geography limitations, impair the economic benefits of shared spectrum. Becoming a MEC and NaaS platform provider for new customer segments could enhance utilization of the dominant market position. MNOs could utilize their big data platforms, analytic skills and CEM capabilities to monetize their unique subscriber data for other industries, without jeopardizing the trust of their customers. Brokering telco data and co-creating value by combining it with vertical data will enable MNOs to capture value from context driven business models.

To strengthen market *boundaries* of the business opportunities, established MNOs could leverage their existing infrastructure investments in radio, core, OSS, as well as in the fixed network assets. Furthermore, the 3GPP evolution offers scale and harmonization in investing in and the build-up of spectrum sharing based businesses. MNOs could also try to turn alternative and new local micro operators into co-opetitive partners thru virtualization and XaaS. As the MBB spectrum management in general and novel shared spectrum initiatives in particular are highly dependent on spectrum policy and regulatory actions, it is essential to play active role in regulation and standardization, and to have direct contact with the national regulator. E.g., in order to protect own entry to new local area collaborative business opportunities, and to keep entry barrier for new non-MNO entrants, MNOs could try delay the introduction of neutral host enabling technologies like MulteFire. As MulteFire could utilize license by rule GAA spectrum, cable companies, Internet Service Providers (ISPs), small businesses, enterprises, venue owners and building owners, can readily deploy it. For new entrants, it offers the chance to own and control their own 'standalone' LTE network. It also offers a number of benefits, including outdoor coverage, wide coverage and improved performance and safety of data and voice applications.

Priority rules help a MNO to identify and rank emerging opportunity. For MNOs, key decision priority is to retain control over the spectrum, and prefer CR network techniques and solution that keep control in the operator domain. Having spectrum control integrated with the OSS NMS enables a MNO to utilize its advanced HetNet SON features, and to protect operation critical network information. Spectrum sharing could start first with other domains like federal users in the case of the CBRS. Furthermore, from the regulatory perspectives, it is central to keep sharing voluntary and binary with the incumbent. At the early stages of spectrum sharing businesses, a MNO will appreciate premium Average Revenue Per User (ARPU) services over operational efficiency to utilize their customer base. In the second phase, MNOs could explore value co-capture opportunities with verticals and other industry domains.

Synchronization, coordination and *timing* of emerging opportunities is the fourth simple rule category. In-house HetNet intersystem spectrum sharing could be implemented first in order to develop needed dynamic capabilities to optimize utilization of spectrum resources across layers. In order to leverage existing business models, operators should prioritize the QoS guaranteed and predictable PAL sharing opportunities first. Offering could then be complement with offloading and local sharing at the GAA layers with better QoS compared traditional Wi-Fi offloading. Thirdly, with full set of spectrum assets a MNO could explore opportunities with local alternative operators and verticals utilizing wholesale, XaaS, MEC and data brokering platforms.

Finally, *Exit rules* help in identifying basis for exit, or initiatives to be stopped. Regardless of the technology enablers or business models utilized in spectrum sharing, MNOs should never give up spectrum, even if not fully utilized. MNOs should try to avoid co-primary sharing concepts that introduce sharing between MNOs, which may have negative impact on their competitive positioning, and the availability of the exclusive spectrum in the future. In the CBRS FCC regulation [7], the term *unused* is important as according to FCC rules GAA users may utilize unused PAL spectrum if unused. Furthermore, exclusive spectrum will remain first priority having important strategic value in keeping the entry barrier for new entrant high and protecting high investments in spectrum and infrastructure.

TABLE II. SUMMARY OF DEVELOPED SIMPLE RULES

Opportunities	*How to rules*	*Boundary rules*	*Priority rules*	*Timing rules*	*Exit rules*
Premium connectivity service to existing customer base with growing demand Premium connectivity with extra capacity and *mobile edge computing* Wholesale and *NaaS* offering to focused market demand based on access to local lower-cost spectrum Telco *data monetization* with verticals locally	Invest to maintain dominant market position Gain access to all exclusive spectrum available Strengthen existing customer lock-in Utilize shared CBRS spectrum assets to deliver premium and localized services Become edge computing and XaaS platform provider for new customer segments Broker telco data to enter verticals with context	Leverage existing infrastructure Utilize scale and harmonization of 3GPP evolution Active lobbying and contribution to regulation Delay the introduction of neutral host technologies to keep entry barrier Turn alternative operators to co-opetitive partners thru virtualization and XaaS.	Maintain control over spectrum Protect operation critical network information Prioritize sharing with other domains Keep sharing voluntary and binary with the incumbent Appreciate premium ARPU services Actively look value capture opportunities in verticals and other industry domains	Base sharing with others on in-house HetNet dynamic capabilities (inter-system sharing and optimization first) QoS guaranteed and predictable PAL sharing Offloading and local sharing at GAA layers Explore opportunities with local alternative operators	Exclusive spectrum is first priority Avoid co-primary sharing concepts between MNOs Protect critical operational network data Monetize customer and telco data

In the MNO strategic decision making, strategic value may in many case overrule technology based avoided cost engineering value and business driven market surplus value. Protection of the critical operational network data remains important source of competitive advantage. Entering co-opetitive business with other industries with content and context based business models; customer and telco data will become critical assets, and create competitive advantage when optimally combined with the use case specific vertical data, or Internet company's customer data assets

VI. CONCLUSION AND FUTURE WORK

This paper discussed the transformative role of the novel Citizen Broadband Radio Service framework in the future mobile broadband networks as an endeavor to meet the growing traffic demand and changing consumption characteristics of the customers while paving the way to make licensed spectrum sharing a third mainstream way of licensing spectrum to commercial users complementing traditional exclusive licensing and unlicensed spectrum access. We utilized co-opetitive business opportunity framework for understanding mobile network operator's enablers and opportunities and how they are framed from policy, technology, and business perspectives, in the future CBRS shared spectrum networks. Opportunity analysis was used in creating and discussing strategic options as simple rules.

We argue that policy and regulation will be on the one hand the key enablers in the path toward shared spectrum access, and on the other hand will play key role in removing limiting and challenging elements critical in the first steps of that path. In particular, the sharing framework for the priority access licenses should be attractive and feasible to encourage mobile broadband industry to invest, which could lower the barrier for change, and furthermore create economies of scale across tiers and for the whole ecosystem.

More flexible and scalable use of the spectrum aims to increase the efficiency of spectrum use in delivering fast growing and converging mobile broadband, media and Internet content to meet changing consumer needs. The proposed opportunities and related simple rules enable mobile network operators to retain existing customers, acquire new customers and strengthen overall market position by offering improved personalized mobile broadband data services timely. Furthermore, through unbundling investment in spectrum, network infrastructure and services co-operative business opportunities may open with vertical segments, new alternative operator types and the Internet domain.

Mobile operators are optimally positioned towards these business opportunities in parallel with their traditional business model leveraging technology enablers from mobile broadband 3GPP LTE evolution and big data analytics while waiting for the more optimized cognitive 5G solutions.

This paper serves as a starting point for analyzing the business enablers, opportunities and business environment around the CBRS. We saw that the concept of co-opetition could be used to characterize the business environment regarding spectrum sharing. The strategic choices as simple rules provides a dynamic framework for MNOs for exploring and exploiting emerging opportunities, developing dynamic capabilities to respond transforming environment, and building business models to leverage new shared spectrum access approaches. However, future work is needed to expand research to cover also other key stakeholders, in particular alternative new local operators, and to dwell deeper into the framework of value co-creation, co-capture and co-opetition for identifying MNOs' business models and ecosystem relations in the new CBRS concept and in the third opportunistic GAA layer in particular.

ACKNOWLEDGMENTS

This work is supported by Tekes – the Finnish Funding Agency for Technology and Innovation. The author would like to acknowledge CORE++ project consortium: VTT Technical Research Centre of Finland, University of Oulu, Centria University of Applied Sciences, Turku University of Applied Sciences, Nokia, PehuTec, Bittium, Anite, Finnish Defence Forces and Finnish Communications Regulatory Authority.

REFERENCES

[1] S. Yrjölä, "Citizens Broadband Radio Service Spectrum Sharing Framework - A Path to New Business Opportunity for Mobile Network Operators?," In Proc. The Sixth International Conference on Advances in Cognitive Radio (COCORA), Lisbon, 2016.

[2] The White House: Realizing the Full Potential of Government-Held Spectrum to Spur Economic Growth. President's Council of Advisors on Science and Technology (PCAST) Report, 2012.

[3] Cisco white paper: Cisco Visual Networking Index: Global Mobile Data Traffic Forecast Update, 2014–2019. [Online]. Available from: http://www.cisco.com/c/en/us/solutions/collateral/service-provider/visual-networking-index-vni/white_paper_c11-520862.html 2016.11.04

[4] FCC: White Spaces. [Online]. Available from: http://www.fcc.gov/topic/white-space 2016.11.04.

[5] Ofcom: TV White Spaces Pilot. [Online]. Available from: http://stakeholders.ofcom.org.uk/spectrum/tv-white-spaces/white-spaces-pilot/ 2016.11.04

[6] ECC: Licensed Shared Access (LSA). ECC Report 205, 2014.

[7] FCC: Report and Order and second FNPRM to advance availability of 3550-3700 MHz band for wireless broadband, 2015.

[8] J. Chapin and W. Lehr, "Cognitive radios for dynamic spectrum access – The path to market success for dynamic spectrum access technology," IEEE Commun. Mag., vol. 45, no. 5, 2007, pp. 96-103.

[9] M. Matinmikko et al., "Business benefits of Licensed Shared Access (LSA) for key stakeholders," In O. Holland, H. Bogucka & A. Medeisis (eds.) Opportunistic Spectrum Sharing and White Space Access: The Practical Reality. John Wiley & Sons, 2015.

[10] P. Ahokangas, M. Matinmikko, S. Yrjölä, H. Okkonen, and T. Casey, ""Simple rules" for mobile network operators' strategic choices in future cognitive spectrum sharing networks," IEEE Wireless Communications, vol.20, no.2, 2013, pp. 20-26.

[11] S. Yrjölä, P. Ahokangas, and M. Matinmikko, "Evaluation of recent spectrum sharing concepts from business model scalability point of view," in Proc. IEEE DySPAN, Stockholm, 2015, pp. 241-250.

[12] S. Yrjölä, M. Matinmikko, M. Mustonen, and P. Ahokangas, "Analysis Of Dynamic Capabilities In The Citizens Broadband Radio Service," in Proc. Wireless Innovation Forum Conference on Wireless Communication Technologies and Software Defined Radio (WInnComm '16), Reston, 2015.

[13] K.M. Eisenhardt, D.M. Sull, "Strategy as simple rules," Harvard Business Review, vol. 79, no. 1, 2001, pp. 107-116.

[14] The White House: Expanding America's Leadership in Wireless Innovation. Presidential Memorandum, 2013.

[15] The WINNF Spectrum Sharing Committee, "SAS Functional Architecture," [Online]. Available from: http://groups.winnforum.org/d/do/8512 2016.11.04

[16] The WINNF Spectrum Sharing Committee. [Online]. Available from: http://www.wirelessinnovation.org/spectrum-sharing-committee 2016.11.04.

[17] D. Hansen, R. Shrader, and J. Monllor, "Defragmenting Definitions of Entrepreneurial Opportunity, Journal of Small Business Mgmnt," vol 49, no. 2, 2011, pp. 283-304.

[18] J. West, "Value Capture and Value Networks in open source vendor strategies," In: Proc. of the 40th Annual Hawasection International Conference on System Sciences, 2007.

[19] A. Brandenburger and B. Nalebuff, "Co-opetition," New York: Doubleday, 1998.

[20] B. Wirtz, O. Schilke, and S. Ullrich, "Strategic development of business models – implications of the web 2.0 for creating value on the Internet," Long Range Planning, Vol. 43, 2010, pp.272–290.

[21] M. Porter, "The Five Competitive Forces That Shape Strategy," Harvard business Review, 2008.

[22] C.K. Prahalad and G. Hamel, "The core competence of the corporation," Harvard Business Review, 68(3), 1990, pp. 79–91.

[23] 3GPP: Technical report TR 36.808: Evolved Universal Terrestrial Radio Access (E-UTRA); Carrier Aggregation; Base Station (BS) radio transmission and reception," 2012.

[24] 3GPP: Study on Licensed-Assisted Access using LTE. RP-141646, 2014.

[25] Qualcomm, "Introducing MuLTEfire: LTE-like performance with Wi-Fi-like simplicity," [Online]. Available from: https://www.qualcomm.com/news/onq/2015/06/11/introducing-multefire-lte-performance-wi-fi-simplicity 2016.11.04

[26] 3GPP: Telecommunication management; Principles and high level requirement. 3GPP TS 32.101 V12.0.0 [Rel-12], 2014.

[27] ETSI: Mobile Edge Computing [Online]. Available from: http://www.etsi.org/technologies-clusters/technologies/mobile-edge-computing 2016.11.04

[28] A. Stephany, "The Business of Sharing: Making it in the New Sharing Economy," Palgrave and Macmillan, 2015.

Possibilities of Quality of Service Parameter Tracking and Transformation in Industrial Applications

György Kálmán

Centre for Cyber and Information Security
Critical Infrastructure Protection Group
Norwegian University of Science and Technology
mnemonic AS
Email: gyorgy.kalman@ntnu.no

***Abstract*—Machine to machine communication offers both an opportunity and poses a challenge for communication networks. In this paper, after an introduction to industrial control networks, an overview of typical QoS metrics is given and their relation to automation metrics is analyzed, current industrial networking technologies and their QoS possibilities are presented. Conversion or mapping of QoS metrics between communication and control systems is evaluated. As a possible direction, use of formal methods and procedures known from industrial safety systems are recommended.**

***Keywords*—critical infrastructure; QoS; metrics; automation; control networks; PROFINET; EtherCAT; Ethernet.**

I. Introduction

This paper is an extension of [1], "Quality of Service Parameter Tracking and Transformation in Industrial Applications," published at IARIA AICT 2016.

Since the introduction of packet switched networks, questions and analyses around the possible service level have been a hot topic. In current networks, the use of best-effort forwarding is dominating. Although it is very efficient, guaranteeing end-to-end connection parameters is a challenge and currently mostly done by overprovisioning.

The technology landscape is similar in both office or communication and industrial networks: on the Local Area Network (LAN) field, Ethernet is dominating, on the Wide Area Network (WAN) side, standard telecommunication solutions are used also for industrial applications.

Since its introduction in industrial automation, Ethernet's determinism has been a returning concern, mainly because of both outdated information (behavior of 10-Base2) and bus-like topologies [2] with long chains of switches.

Most of the bandwidth-related problems were solved with the introduction of gigabit Ethernet and for the most demanding applications, technologies like EtherCAT, with intrinsic QoS are available. For traditional switched networks, there are efforts for the inclusion of a resource management plane in the IEEE 802.1 Time-Sensitive Networking Task Group (TSN).

The paper is structured as follows: the second section gives an introduction to industrial control networks, the third section gives an overview of QoS. Section four gives an overview on QoS features of current networking technologies used, section five provides an overview of Distributed Control System (DCS) structures. Section VI presents how requirements may be specified in a structured way, Section VII explains the importance of requirements tracking. Section VIII presents parameters of a control loop and how QoS parameters can be converted between the industrial and communication metrics. Section IX draws the conclusion and provides an outlook on future work.

II. Industrial Control Networks

In a historical perspective, control of manufacturing and process plants was done mechanically: the transmission of signals were done by some physical mean, like pneumatics, hydraulics or manual force. These mechanical structures were replaced by electric solutions in parts of the systems. Electric control had been successful and mechanical control systems were replaced by electronics, mostly employing hardwired circuits [3].

The hardwired circuits were both prone to errors and consumed large amounts of space and money. A similar evolution has happened as with the telecommunication lines: a digital, interleaved solution was needed [4].

With the introduction of microelectronics and digital bus systems, it became possible to exchange the long and expensive dedicated wiring with bus systems, commonly called as fieldbus. We can date the birth of QoS in industrial environments to this step of the evolution: in case of direct wiring, there was no question on access to the transmission media. Delay or jitter were not applicable, the signal propagated with nearly the speed of light and had dedicated media (bandwidth) to the controller.

The use of digital communication solutions has spread on all levels of automation and resulted in the current state, where Ethernet is used in both industrial and connected corporate networks. The main difference remaining in these, similar looking networks is the requirements posed by the communication parties. An industrial network is connected to the physical world and events on communicated on this network have a physical dimension. This connection results in different priorities for QoS [5], [6].

Practically all new industrial deployments will use a communication technology, in the vast majority of cases, Ethernet. Each industry has its own set of different, but similar requirements. On the timescale basis, we typically distinguish between: bus bar protection/motion control, manufacturing and process control.

Bus bar protection and motion control require the most stringent achieved QoS levels: the information must reach its destination with great precision and low latency.

Manufacturing has a typical requirement time scale of tens of milliseconds. In the view of corporate networks these requirements are still hard to keep, but in an industrial environment, on this level standard equipment is used. The main support property for the QoS parameter calculation is that the typical source-destination of a control loop with hard requirements is in most of the cases close to each other. As a result, the network as a whole does not have to adhere for the requirements, but paths on the network might be involved.

Process control is the most relaxed of the three and typically poses no strict requirements. In case of a process control loop, the typical timing possibilities are in the second range rather than milliseconds, so delays on current Ethernet networks (which are in the microsecond range) are mostly not noticeable in such installations.

Due to that industrial networks do have a connection to the physical world, failure of such a system has the potential for much more severe impact than that of a corporate system. Effects of failure can be, e.g., damage to equipment, production loss, environmental damage or the worst: injury or loss of life. The connection to physical processes also introduces the need for real-time behavior. The expression real-time is often used as a synonym to *fast*, but the more precise definition is that the network has to give an answer within a specified (real/physical) time slot and if it fails, the data is or nearly is worthless [7], [8].

The strict requirements on delay or jitter are in a reverse order compared to closeness to the physical process: fieldbus tend to have strong requirements, especially if functions, like motion control is executed. The communication after the controller level is less critical, as here mainly the communication parties are the historians and the Human Machine Interface (HMI) units. As in these upper levels, human operators are the typical recipient of information, the expected delays due to traffic and non-determinism are magnitudes smaller than the reaction time of the employees.

Determinism is a property, which, beside telecommunication networks, is not typically used as a measure of QoS. In an industrial environment, it can be one of the questions which need to be answered. Here again, in parallel with jitter and delay, the typical determinism requirements are more strict closer to the physical process. To call a network *deterministic*, it must be possible to give an upper bound for delivering a chunk of data (Fig. 1). In dedicated wire solutions or slotted technologies, like serial lines or bus like Profibus, the upper bound could be calculated from the network setup. In particular, early Ethernet is not a good solution to provide upper bounds. Half-duplex implementations suffered the well-known loss of throughput in high-traffic situations, because of the Carrier Sense Multiple Access with Collision Detection (CSMA/CD) medium access protocol. This history still limits the acceptance of Ethernet in automation environments, however, in current networks with full-duplex switched topologies, CSMA/CD is not needed as there are no collisions. Still, if not media access, traffic situations can lead to queueing. In a typical situation, where the two end-hops are running on 100Mbps, while the backbone network is running on 1Gbps, the accumulated queueing delay after several core hops will be still magnitude lower than the propagation delay of the 100Mbps (non-congested) hops.

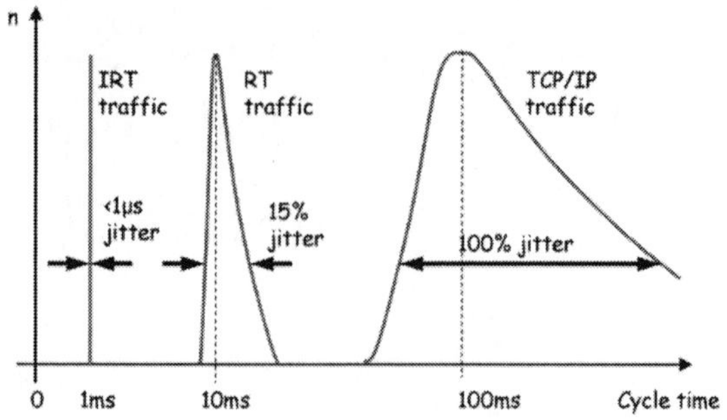

Fig. 1. Delay and jitter ranges in PROFINET [9]

Jitter is the variance of delay. In a network, where a control loop is run, it is typically a requirement to have low jitter, thus the periods of sampling will be uniformly distributed over time. Here the network has to provide a jitter below the upper bound, which is acceptable for the control loop. Time synchronization is one of the features, which provide the connection point towards the physical world. Temporal consistency and the ability to record the events in correct order are important both for supervisory tasks but also for troubleshooting.

An important measure of the network equipment is the throughput. Industrial applications here also have different emphasis areas: in office or telecom, a typical frame has a long payload compared to the header (with the one famous exception being Asynchronous Transfer Mode (ATM)). Data frames transmitted on industrial networks are typically short, especially close to the physical process, where the other QoS requirements are high. This property makes fulfilling the QoS parameters more problematic, as it is easier to utilize the full bandwidth for network equipment if the frames are long, thus fewer forwarding decisions need to be taken and the overhead is also smaller.

Composition of traffic in control networks, especially on the field level, differs considerably from the typical office environment. As the communicating parties are near exclusively machines and the operation of control systems is very often periodic, it is very typical to have a nearly static traffic picture with mostly very stable packet streams. Aperiodic events like state changes or alarm conditions compose a growing part of the traffic starting from being nearly negligible on the field level to being a considerable part on the client-server or plant level. Periodic traffic on the field level was expected to be be problematic, if strict real time requirements are extended with high data speed, like in the case of IEC 61850-sampled values. Experience shows that in most cases, the best effort forwarding works without causing problems, as in typical cases, the offered bandwidth is well above the requirements of the control loop. For special requirements, industrial Ethernet variants, like EtherCAT and Profinet IRT were developed. These offer intrinsic QoS witch scheduling functions supported by the special hardware implementations.

Compared to office networks, a distinct physical feature of the industrial deployments is the ruggedness of devices. A typical device has to withstand vibration, shock, has to accept wider operational and storage temperature ranges and might even need to withstand moisture. From the operational viewpoint, however, these properties have little impact. On the performance side, current chipsets are providing adequate resources even with only using passive cooling and if needed, special connectors are used to avoid physical damage on the connecting wires. The designed lifetime of the devices is much higher than in the office environment: a representative life expectation is around 20 years.

A. Types of Information

On a typical industrial network, there are a handful types of data: control information, related to keeping the process under control, the sampled data, which connects the control system with the physical process, diagnostics and management and auxiliary functions like technical safety.

Control information and process data is the communication between instruments and controller and are the main connection of the control system to the physical world. In most cases, the majority of traffic is part of this category and often the only considered part of the traffic mix. The hard QoS parameters are typically property of traffic in this category, as this layer of the network is the closest of the actual process. Example traffic on this level is sampled values from some instrument, like an Intelligent Electronic Device (IED) or temperature/pressure sensor. Event-controlled traffic is also present, for example, valve status changes.

Diagnostics and management are important auxiliaries: diagnostics is an integral part of creating a reliable control system. Errors of various causes can happen in the system and an effective diagnostics can predict or identify failed components. The detail of diagnostics and the capabilities provided by this subsystem depend on the reliability and redundancy requirements. Diagnostics is a type of data, which is collected by the system, but by default, for expected values, there is no reaction. High coverage diagnostics is also an enabler, for example, Safety Instrumented Systems (SIS). Management of the system is necessary above the very basic level. The overview of current system status is important information for both operators and engineers.

Safety is the most important auxiliary function. A dimension of running a SIS is to have adequate diagnostics. Categories of safety levels are defined by IEC 61508. Safety information is carried in parallel to control information. The different Safety Integrity Levels (SIL) have different implications on redundancy of the safety system and the coverage of diagnostics.

III. Quality of Service

QoS is the measure of transmission quality and service availability of a network [11], thus not only limited to actual forwarding parameters like bandwidth and delay, but also, e.g., availability, reconfiguration time and reliability.

Keeping a certain service level was a requirement in telecommunication networks and it was a natural decision to have features to support service level definition when packet switched networks were introduced in the telecom networks.

Providing QoS in Local Area Networks (LANs) was focused on services, where at least one of the communicating parties was a human. The services could range from web browsing through VoIP to multi-party video conferencing. The parameters were adopted to the human perception and also tolerance for disturbances was adapted to the human users. The metrics for service quality were not new either at that time; telecommunication networks had service levels defined already and since those were also technical and focused on human users, the introduced metrics were also adapted to computer networks, like Ethernet or more generally, Internet Protocol (IP). In current industrial applications, IPv4 is generally used, if needed, then as IPv4 islands interconnected with tunnels over IPv6 networks. In Internet of Things (IoT) installations, the use of IPv6 is expected as a result of the large number of connected devices.

The evolution of technology showed that in the vast majority of cases, an over dimensioning of the network resources is both the cheapest and easiest to manage.

A. Telecommunication metrics

As an example, ATM metrics for traffic contracts are composed from traffic parameters such as:

- *Peak Cell Rate (PCR)* The maximum allowable rate at which cells can be transported along a connection in the ATM network. The PCR is the determining factor in how often cells are sent in relation to time in an effort to minimize jitter.
- *Sustainable Cell Rate (SCR)* A calculation of the average allowable, long-term cell transfer rate on a specific connection.

- *Maximum Burst Size (MBS)* The maximum allowable burst size of cells that can be transmitted contiguously on a particular connection.

and QoS parameters,

- *Cell Transfer Delay (CTD)* The delay experienced by a cell between the time it takes for the first bit of the cell to be transmitted by the source and the last bit of the cell to be received by the destination. Maximum Cell Transfer Delay (Max CTD) and Mean Cell Transfer Delay (Mean CTD) are used.
- *Peak-to-peak Cell Delay Variation (CDV)* The difference between the maximum and minimum CTD experienced during the connection. Peak-to-peak CDV and Instantaneous CDV are used.
- *Cell Loss Ratio (CLR)* The percentage of cells that are lost in the network due to error or congestion and are not received by the destination.

The list shows the focus areas of QoS already in the 90s: bandwidth (in bits per second), burstiness and parameters related to disturbances in forwarding.

In addition to these connection-related parameters, the communication network had also network-wide parameters in other relations, like redundancy with, e.g., reconfiguration time in case of link loss or routing alternatives.

ATM is raised as an example, since it offers one of the widest range of possibilities for QoS. It also introduced a couple of concepts, which, although ATM was later deemed as a failure, do a comeback in today's QoS networks.

B. Metrics on packet switched networks

On packet switched networks, initially the focus was on efficient forwarding. Efficiency and simple network operation lead to cheaper devices and ultimately to today's technology landscape with the domination of Ethernet and IP.

While there were different approaches for QoS (integrated and differentiated services), the main QoS metrics were bandwidth, loss, delay and jitter [11]. In future installations with IPv6 it is expected that the use of differentiated services will be more widespread, as after RFC 2460/3697, the properties of Traffic Class and Flow Label can be used to select flows of the aggregated traffic and grant priority. The 20 bit field of Flow Label also allows a large number of flows to be present concurrently, which would fit even a large industrial deployment. The impact of this feature however depends on the timing of tasks running on the network and also how this field could be used for other properties important in the automation applications: redundancy and reconfiguration time in case of link loss.

An effort to include some of the traffic engineering possibilities of ATM for LANs is the IEEE Shortest Path Bridging (SPB). This standard is being developed by the TSN working group and allows, amongst others call admission, resource reservation over the whole path. SPB has raised a high interest in the automation field and most of the industry is either contributing directly or closely following the development.

C. Automation

QoS requirements of an automation system tend to be very different than those of an office network. The protocol set used is different and the typical communication inside an automation system runs on Layer 2 [12]. Sources and sinks of traffic streams are typically machines with little tolerance on disturbances, but good predictability in communication.

The network topology of automation networks is often contributing to the challenges around QoS [13]. Networks are built with low port count switches. This typically results in an infrastructure that has more devices than an office network. A bigger refinery can have several hundreds of switches with a typical branching factor of 4-7. The still widely used bus-topology leads to even longer forwarding chain, introducing delay and jitter, which only exists in considerably larger networks in the office/telecommunication scenarios.

IV. QoS FEATURES OF INDUSTRIAL ETHERNET

Industrial Ethernet variants are mostly building their QoS features on the existing traffic prioritization services of Ethernet. While not directly a QoS feature, the most important step towards the usability of Ethernet in industrial applications was the introduction of full duplex networks and Ethernet switches.

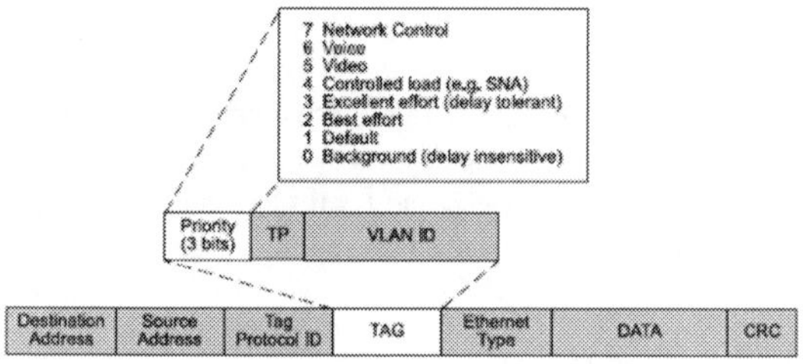

Fig. 2. Ethernet priority field [28]

- *IEEE 802.1p* As the most important traffic management feature, inbuilt in Ethernet. .1p offers the possibility to assign. Priorities have been defined in the project and the switches typically implement a solution with multiple queues and round-robin scheduling with ageing. There are 8 different traffic classes (Fig. 2), from background and best effort up to network control. Unfortunately, in industrial applications, 7 (the highest) is often used. Although this will give these frames priority over all other frames, but since nearly all automation traffic is in the same traffic class, delays might occur. Also, it is not practical that all automation traffic is getting the same priority as the network control, as signaling traffic for the network infrastructure might have much larger impact on the system as the loss of a couple of automation frames.
- *IEEE 802.1 Time Sensitive Networks* TSN is a group of standards, which provides a real-time Ethernet implementation, where deterministic transport of data is possible. In addition to implementing call admission control to guarantee that the communication requirements are fulfilled

through the path, it also introduces a global reference to physical time. The standard has emerged from the IEEE 802.1AVB, Audio-Video Bridging (Fig. 3) proposal and widened the possible field of use with automation and especially the use of Ethernet in the Internet of Things (IoT).

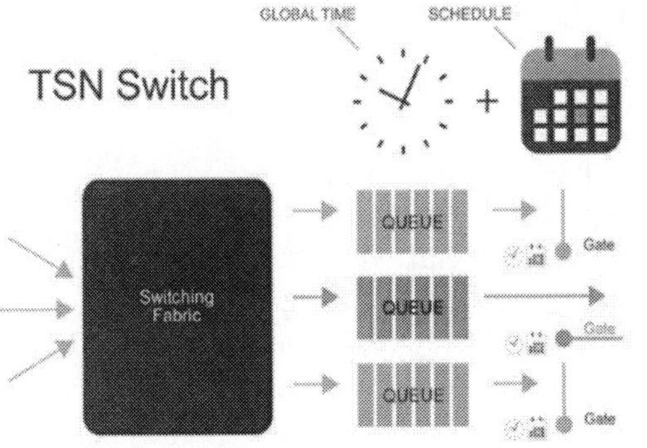

Fig. 3. Connection of physical time and traffic in TSN [14]

A. PROFINET

PROFINET was developed and is the preferred Industrial Ethernet variant of Siemens. The main QoS feature is that by default, PROFINET provides three different traffic classes (Fig. 4: the first one provides a framing service for legacy PROFIBUS and also carries non-critical data with cycle times of around or above 100ms. The traffic can be run on normal TCP/IP. The second traffic class is, what the protocol calls, Real Time (RT), which is supporting IO applications with a cycle time of around 1ms to 100ms [15]. The third traffic

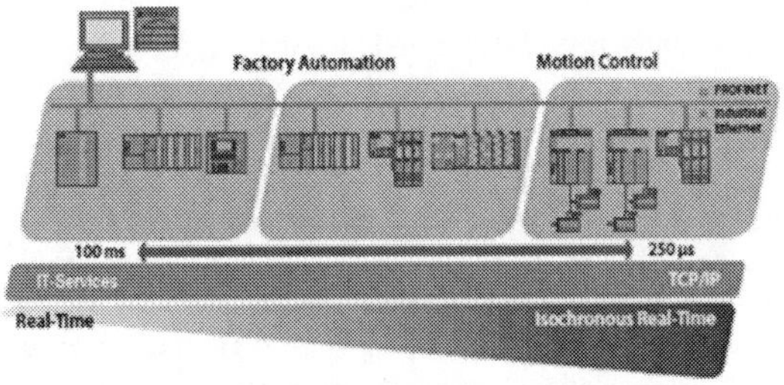

Fig. 4. Traffic classes of PROFINET [16]

class is Isochronous Real Time (IRT). With using special hardware, IRT provides a communication solution for low-latency applications.

B. EtherCAT

EtherCAT was developed to provide a deterministic network solution for devices on a local ring. It is a technology with an intrinsic QoS solution, as the processing of the data on the ring is done on the fly, as the frame travels through the

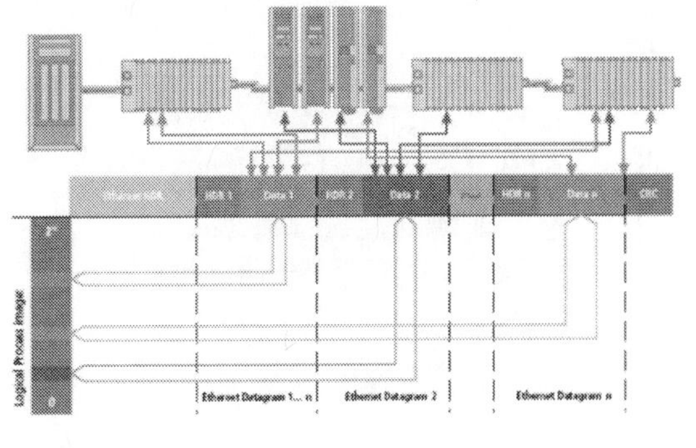

Fig. 5. EtherCAT master-slave example [17]

Application Specific Integrated Circuits (ASICs) of the slave machines (Fig. 5). A representative example of the cycle times is that the master is beginning to receive the frame at its input, before the sending is finished on the output. The simple topology and the call admission control are both enablers to allow the short cycle times. The most important property is the possibility to calculate the cycle time with high precision. An additional flexible feature is that in-between the periodic frames, it is compatible with normal traffic and it is possible to send out these also on the automation loop.

C. SERCOS III

SERCOS III combines a solution resembling EtherCAT for on-the-fly processing of the frames and the possibility to use L3 communication for non-critical information exchange. The slave processing is done as the frame traverses the Ethernet interface, but SERCOS splits the in- and output to different frames as compared to the single frame sent in the case of EtherCAT.

D. IEC 61850

IEC 61850 is implemented directly over L2. This industrial Ethernet type is used mainly in electric substation automation. The traffic itself is typically composed of multicast and unicast frames, the delay and jitter depends on the QoS functions of standard Ethernet. The lack of L3 in the communication stack enables potentially faster communication, reaching the level of the best case Ethernet.

E. Ethernet/Industrial Protocol

Ethernet/IP is a protocol developed by Open DeviceNet Vendors Association (ODVA), led by Rockwell Automation. The Ethernet/IP protocol is implemented on the application layer and provides an encapsulation service for Common Industrial Protocol (CIP) data (Fig. 6). Implementing a protocol on the application layer has both its positive and negative implications. From the QoS viewpoint, the use of application layer allows the utilization of the features offered by lower layers: prioritization on L2 (Ethernet) and IntServ or DiffServ features (if implemented) on L3. The shortcoming of the application layer is that strict, low latency control loops are

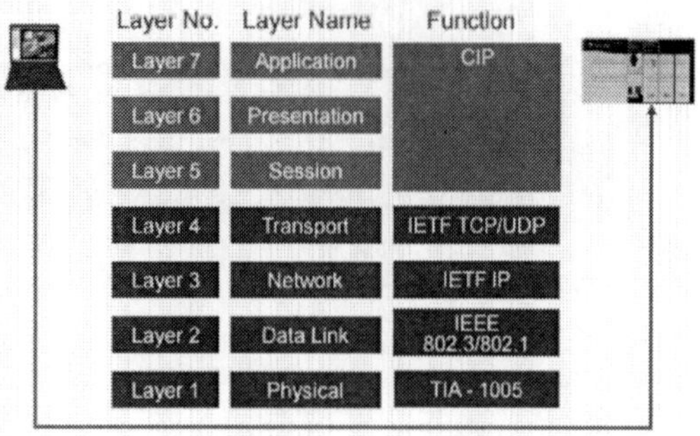

Fig. 6. Protocol stack of Ethernet/IP [18]

in practice not feasible. This is a result of primarily the delay added by the travel through the protocol stack. In an optimal situation, the timing properties can be very close to one of standard Ethernet.

F. Foundation Fieldbus High Speed Ethernet

Foundation Fieldbus HSE is implemented as an application layer protocol and has similar properties and limitations as Ethernet/IP: in the best case, the delay and jitter can be close to the L2-based implementations, but the additional software layers will introduce some uncertainty.

V. DCS ARCHITECTURE

Control systems are traditionally built using a three network levels (Fig. 7.). The plant, the client-server and the control network. These levels might have different names, but they share the following characteristics:

- *Plant network* is home of the traditional IT systems, like Enterprise Resource Planning (ERP), office services and other support applications. It is typically under the control of the IT department.
- Client-server network is the non-time critical part of the automation system, where the process-related workplaces, servers and other support entities are located. It is firewalled from the plant network and is under the control of Operations.
- Control network includes everything close to the actual process: controllers, sensors, actuators and other automation components. Typically, it follows a strict time synchronization regime and contains the parts of the network with time-critical components. It is accessible through proxies from the client-server network and under the control of Operations.

The most important component from the control systems viewpoint is the Programmable Logic Controller (PLC) or controller. These are specialized industrial computers implemented as solid-state electronic devices, they replaced hardwired relay-based circuits. Current devices, beside offering the traditional groups of digital and analogue circuit interfaces towards instrumentation, also offer a wide range of other services, like logging, status report over SNMP or security features like a firewall.

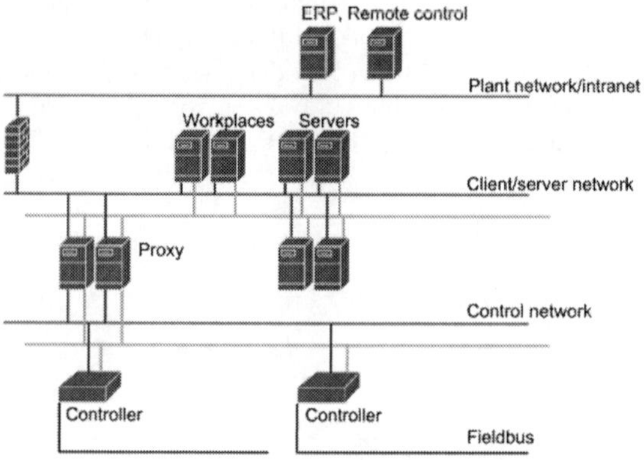

Fig. 7. Traditional DCS network architecture

TABLE I
COMPARISON OF DCS AND SCADA PROPERTIES

SCADA	*DCS*
Small physical distances	Large distances
Independent system	Interconnects/monitors several systems
Full local network control	Typically uses third parties
Data driven	Event driven

Remote monitoring was introduced to industrial applications decades ago with the different Supervisory Control and Data Acquisition (SCADA) systems. These used various communication technologies (leased lines, radio links, etc.) to feed in status data to a central monitoring entity. Typically, remote control was not available. SCADA operations can be very much represented as a software-only entity. Since SCADA only has the task to supervise the selected systems, the communication is less critical and mostly event-driven. Remote Terminal Units (RTUs) are used to feed the data to the central entity, the Master Terminal Unit (MTU). Remote monitoring is not a replacement for functionality on site: operations shall be possible to maintain also in island mode. SCADA is not expected to lower the site's reliability or security [19], [20]. The typical long physical extent requires the use of communication infrastructure delivered of third parties. The cost pressure on the communication costs typically led also in these operations to move from leased lines or other high QoS-high cost solutions to packet switched solutions.

Developments in the smart grid and IoT extend the possibilities for remote operations is by taking current communication solutions in use. The extension of the features also requires a well-defined network infrastructure [21]. An interesting aspect from the interconnecting task of SCADA systems is that the typical hardware/software platform used for the SCADA system will be obsolete in a couple of years, and will be needed to be upgraded, the systems the SCADA is reporting abbot will still have the same, relatively old DSC as clients.

A. QoS in automation

Traffic flows in automation typically are M2M. This property and the systems connectivity to the physical world require both different tolerances for disturbances and potentially different metrics [22].

An automation system somewhere in the process is connected to the physical world even if some of the functions can be virtualized [23]. This means that amongst others, it has to refer to real time. Forwarding disturbances might lead to potentially dangerous situations with implications far beyond a dropped Voice over Internet Protocol (VoIP) call.

The definition of QoS requirements in the automation world has its roots in the definition of control loops. In control of the early DCSs bus and serial links were used, which typically operated in a slotted or polled way. This allowed the automation engineers to exactly set the communication parameters to meet the requirements of the control system in a deterministic way.

For special applications, technologies with intrinsic QoS are used, e.g., EtherCAT, which allows deterministic communication, but represents a minority of installations. In the following, focus will be on solutions, where no intrinsic QoS is available.

The physical world connection also has an influence on the used QoS metrics. In automation, beside bandwidth, time and availability related metrics are more emphasized, like delay and jitter or availability (redundancy, reconfiguration time). A special aspect is also the quality of time synchronization. The importance and weighting of these metrics is different compared to the telecommunication or other communication operations. One of the most important differences is that at the moment there is no protocol which would bridge the gap between requirements specification in automation terms and network operations, which results in extended engineering work and challenging life-cycle support. This is in contrast with, e.g., VoIP, where protocols like the Resource Reservation Protocol (RSVP) can be used to reserve resources on the communication path.

VI. Requirements specification

Defining requirements and keeping the original intention in complex systems is a problematic task. In automation, the main challenge is that the requirements are defined in the automation context, but the bearer network uses by default different metrics for expressing forwarding parameters.

In a control loop, typical parameters are control frequency (how often the data is refreshed or modified), maximum tolerable delay, jitter and availability parameters. One of the most demanding applications, where no technology with intrinsic QoS is used is substation automation with IEC 61850 [24].

IEC 61850 is a standard for communication networks and systems for power utility automation. This protocol is a great step forward for substation automation, as it, amongst others translates all information into data models, which is supported by the application focused architecture. This speeds up the engineering process both in planning and integration [25].

However, also IEC 61850 is not defining exact QoS requirements for the network infrastructure. Although the Specific Communication Service Mapping (SCSM) feature allows the definition of communication links inside the IEC 61850 world, the translation of requirements is not included.

When the control loops are defined, the current process is based on individual mapping of automation requirements to network QoS parameters. This process, although not efficient, can and is working for smaller installations, but suffers from scalability problems. The lack of direct coupling between the automation and communication parameters typically leads to very pessimistic QoS requirements.

In the Internet of Things (IoT) scenario, where the automation networks are extended behind the LAN [26], tracking requirements is becoming more important. Very strict parameters of the automation system on the LAN can be mixed into the WAN requirements, which might lead to prohibitive cost on communication. Validity of requirements for each flow has to be analyzed to ensure an efficient fit. The efforts for keeping the QoS parameters as close to the requirements as possible can lead to more efficient and cheaper operation.

A. Industrial safety

Conversations on Safety Integrated Systems (SIS) mainly include questions on QoS. The cause is that these installations share the communication network between the automation task and the safety function (as they can also share infrastructure with the fire alarm system). In a safety sense, SIS have no QoS requirements. The safety logic is built in a way, so that a communication error is interpreted as a dangerous situation and the safety function will trip. So, the system avoids dangerous situations at the expense of lower productivity and availability.

Safety as such is an availability question and through availability, it implies QoS requirements on the automation system as any other communication task. Special treatment is not required.

Although a solution like this does not exist for communication QoS, but the industry has a field, where a similar challenge was solved with structured approach and formal methods: safety. Safety is already considered as a process, which is present for the whole life cycle of the product.

Safety systems are classified into 4 levels, Safety Integrity Level (SIL) 1 to 4. The different levels pose well-defined requirements towards the system. These integrity levels cover all aspects of the system, including hardware, software, communication solution and seen in contrast with the application. A similar approach could be also beneficial for formalizing the relationship between the automation application and the bearer network.

The IEC 61508 standard requires that each risk posed by the components of the safety system is identified and analyzed. The result of the risk analysis should be evaluated against tolerability criteria.

Key processes of a safety development are risk analysis and risk reduction. These are executed in an iterative manner

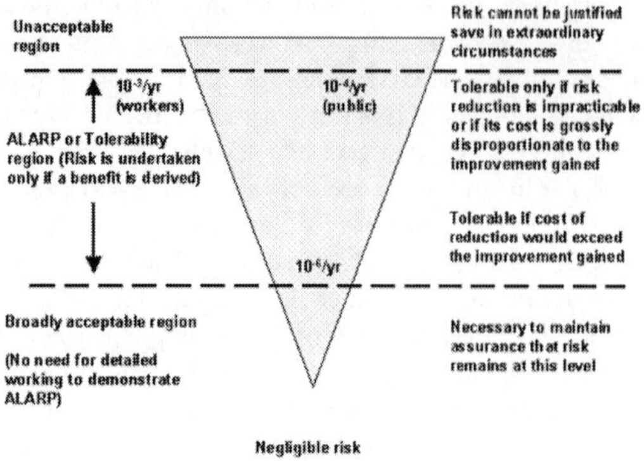

Fig. 8. The Health and Safety Executive's Risk criteria

	Requirement 1	Requirement 2	Requirement 3	Requirement 4	Requirement 5	...	...	...	...	...	...	...	...	...	...	...	...	Requirement n
Subsystem 1	x			x														
Subsystem 2		x			x													
Subsystem 3			x			...	...	...	...	...	...	...	...	...	...	...	...	
...						...	...	...	...	...	...	...	...	...	...	...	...	
...						...	...	...	...	...	...	...	...	...	...	...	...	
...						...	...	...	...	...	...	...	...	...	...	...	...	
Subsystem n																		x

Fig. 9. Requirements traceability matrix by the U.S. Department of Transportation

until the acceptable risk level is achieved. A possible method for risk classification is shown on Fig. 8. from the United Kingdom Health and Safety Executive.

Analogue to this, a similar approach could be used for defining an operational envelope for the communication infrastructure. All possible flows of data should be identified (analogue with identifying risk), which is possible with high confidence on a mostly M2M communication system. Then these flows should be analyzed and as a result, QoS requirements for the flows should be identified. As these are identified, the aggregated results should be evaluated against the possibilities of the underlying infrastructure [27].

The analysis will result in a range, stating the minimum QoS requirement (with a certain confidence) and the preferred QoS requirement. If the expected QoS after taking communication flows into account is inside the operational envelope, the system can deliver with the defined confidentiality level.

The operational envelope will be larger than zero (not just forming a baseline composed from the single QoS requirements) because of the stochastic nature of best-effort forwarding and large networks. Also, an analogy with the different SIL can be drawn with comparing them to the confidentiality level of keeping the Service Level Agreement (SLA) [29].

The approach taken for safety can be a solution for other properties of the industrial communication system, e.g., QoS for transport or security [30].

VII. Requirements Tracking

One of the key aspects missing in engineering work today is the follow-up of requirements stated against the communication infrastructure.

On the LAN level, the lack of tracking only results in minor problems, as network resources are typically not problematic. Even not on the redundancy requirements, since most of the critical network will have approximately the same reliability requirements. As an example, a current IEC 61850 substation will have tens of devices connected to the network.

The local communication of IEC 61850 is composed from horizontal and vertical flows, where horizontal flows tend to use more resources, as Sampled Values (SV) traffic is sent this way. SV is the continuous stream of sampled input or output values, which is sent to a controller for processing. The stream can fill 10s of Mbps. On a network with a gigabit backhaul, conveying traffic in several 100 Mbps range is not problematic. Redundancy is typically covered by either a secondary network or redundant links.

Already in the horizontal-vertical split of flows, different requirements are valid against the network infrastructure. As the automation task gets more far away from the fieldbus level (direct contact with the physical world), so are the deadlines for communication and processing more relaxed.

Requirements tracking is becoming key as the automation system passes the LAN boundary. Costs associated to network communication are becoming more expensive and obeying QoS parameters increasingly problematic.

Several well-known approaches can help the aggregation and validation of the QoS parameters during the life cycle of the project. One of these solutions is the requirements traceability matrix.

In such a matrix, requirements posed by different automation tasks towards the infrastructure can be gathered (Fig. 9.). To allow both aggregation of parameters and identification of the source of a specific requirement.

Source identification is key for long-life installations, where extensions and updates can be expected during the lifetime of the system.

Evaluation if a requirement is still valid in different parts or domains of the system has also a key importance in efficient deployments. It is important to set up an iterative process for QoS parameter evaluation. Here, a possible solution could be to follow the V-model used in, amongst others, software development and safety development. Fig. 10. shows the iterative development process. The QoS requirements should be evaluated at each step and their fulfilment validated after each step. With using such a model, the bearer infrastructure would be more integrated into the development process. Integration can lead to more optimized QoS requirements. Current practice results more in a worst-case requirement list.

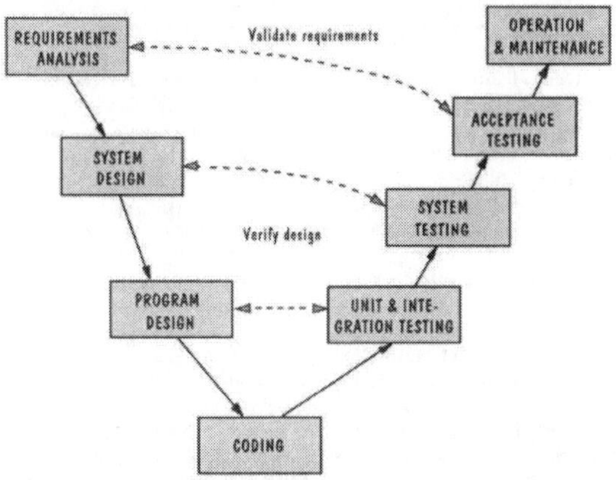

Fig. 10. V-model [31]

For WAN situations, tracking requirement validity has key importance. The validity area of the respective QoS parameters has to be limited to cover only the necessary parts. As part of an iterative process, when the communication scope is getting wider (e.g., the data is being passed upward in a hierarchical network architecture), validity of the QoS parameters has to be checked. An example is that if there is a strict time synchronization requirement with IEEE 1588, but there is no such requirement for the WAN section, nor is a loop covering two endpoints in different networks, then the 1588 requirement should not be taken over to the SLA definition of the WAN interface.

VIII. Control loop parameters

Requirements definition for the communication network is one of the actual challenges in automation. The challenge in this task is that the automation flows are defined using different metrics than the communication links. An example IEC 61850 control loop would be defined as: having a sampling rate of 80 samples per cycle (4800 Hz for 60 Hz networks), with sampling 16 inputs, 16 bit per sample. Event-based traffic is negligible compared to the periodic traffic. If there is a requirement for synchronous operation, time precision (quality) can also be a QoS metric. Redundancy requirements can lead to topologies, which are unusual in a normal network infrastructure: first, the use of Rapid Spanning Tree Protocol (RSTP) to disable redundant links, second the general use of loops (rings) in the network to ensure that all nodes are dual-homed. With dual-homing, the network can survive the loss of one communication link without degradation in the service level. From the network viewpoint, this control loop will introduce a traffic flow, with a net ingress payload stream of approx. 98Mbps. The sampling will generate 2560 bytes of traffic each second, which can be carried by at least two Ethernet frames, thus the system can expect at least approx. 10000 frames per second. The traffic will be forwarded on a horizontal path to the controller. On the ingress port to the backbone, it will enter with approx. 110 Mbps (header+payload). The traffic flow will be consumed at the egress port to the controller.

Due to the stochastic nature of Ethernet, there will be jitter between the frames transmitted over the network. The maximum jitter is defined by the maximum delay variation tolerance of the control loop (typically, every second frame must arrive in good time). This requirement can then be calculated with either the length of the typical frame of the flow or with a maximum length frame. In both cases, the allowed jitter will be considerably longer than the expected disturbances on the LAN. Precision requirement on the time synchronization implies two choices: the choice of protocol and time source. The choice of protocol is generally IEEE 1588v2, which allows high precision time synchronization and GPS as a time source. The choice of GPS is actually an input to the risk analysis of the whole project, as then the time reference will depend on a network controlled by a third party.

IX. Conclusion and future work

With communicating automation systems covering large geographical areas and also expanding in logical complexity, current, non-scalable solutions for performance definition and evaluation are getting outdated. Deterministic mapping of control-related parameters to QoS parameters of the used networking technologies supported with requirements tracking can be a way to go.

To show a similar process in the engineering of automation systems, examples from safety integrated systems are shown. Introduction of the structured approach used in safety development can both enhance the quality of deployments and also allow easier communication between the parties. The main gain with using a process built on the safety development is, that the safety process (like the V-model) is already known and accepted. Networking and QoS is, as safety, not a single delivery, but a process and follows the life-cycle of the product.

Future work will focus on, how QoS requirements can be formalized in a technologically neutral way and mapped into actual solutions. Protocol development or adaptation for resource reservation for automation applications in both LAN and WAN environments is an important field of study, including the use of SDN in automation [10], [32].

As an outlook, future hot spots of research could be automatic parameter tracking through the design process and real time monitoring of deployments also during their operation. Automation and smart grids are an important field of 5G efforts and it is expected to utilize the existing telecommunication protocols with applying industry-specific profiles, including protocols like Resource reSerVation Protocol (RSVP). Developing these profiles which will not only define the infrastructure requirements, but also interfaces towards other systems.

References

[1] Gy. Kálmán, "Quality of Service Parameter Tracking and Transformation in Industrial Applications," in Proceedings of IARIA AICT 2016, St. Julians, Malta

[2] Gy. Kálmán, D. Orfanus, and R. Hussain, "An Overview of Switching Solutions for Wired Industrial Ethernet," The Thirteenth International Conference on Networks ICN 2014, pp. 131-136, Nice

[3] B. Galloway, and G. Hancke, "Introduction to Industrial Control Networks," IEEE Communications Surveys and Tutorials, Volume 15, Issue 2, Pages: 860-880, 2013 Q2

[4] Alcate-Lucent, "Transformation of mission-critical communication networks," Alcatel-Lucent White Paper, 2015

[5] H. Bernhard, and J. Mottok, "Real-time behavior of Ethernet on the example of PROFINET," https://www.hs-regensburg.de/fileadmin/media/fakultaeten/ei/forschung_projekte/MAPR_Ver%C3%B6ffentlichungen/ARC_Heitzer.pdf, accessed: 08.09.2016

[6] Y. Jeon, "QoS Requirements for the Smart Grid Communications System," IJCSNS International Journal of Computer Science and Network Security, Volume 11, Issue 3, 2011

[7] I. Dominguez-Jaimes, L. Wisniewski, and H. Trsek, "Identification of Traffic Flows in Ethernet-based Industrial Fieldbuses," IEEE Emerging Technolgoies and Factory Automation (ETFA), 2010

[8] M. Yaghmaee, Z. Yousefi, M. Zabhi, and S. Alishahi, "Quality of Service Guarantee in Smart Grid Infrastructure Communication Using Traffic Classification," 22nd International Conference on Electricity Distribution, Stockholm, 2013

[9] A. Verwer, "Overview and Applications of PROFINET," PROFIBUS and PROFINET International, http://www.profibus.com/uploads/media/profinet_overview.pdf.pdf, accessed: 08.09.2016

[10] Gy. Kálmán, "Applicability of Software Defined Networking in Industrial Ethernet," in Proceedings of IEEE Telfor 2015, pp. 340-343, Belgrade, Serbia

[11] Cisco, "End-to-End QoS Network Design: Quality of Service for Rich-Media & Cloud Networks," Cisco Press, 2013

[12] C. Alcaraz, G. Fernandez, and F. Carvajal, "Security Aspects of SCADA and DCS Environments," In Critical Infrastructure Protection: Information Infrastructure Models, Analysis, and Defense, LNCS 7130, Springer, 2012, pp. 120-149

[13] L. Sheng, "QoS Design and Its Implementation for Intelligent Industrial Ethernet," International Journal of Materials, Mechanics and Manufacturing, Vol. 4, No. 1, 2016, pp. 40-45.

[14] TTTech, "Deterministic Ethernet and TSN: automotive and industrial IoT," Industrial Ethernet Book, Issue 89/8, 2016

[15] P. Neumann, and A. Pöschmann, "Ethernet-based Real-Time Communications with PROFINET IO," ACMOS'05 Proceedings of the 7th WSEAS international conference on Automatic control, modeling and simulation, Pages 54-61, 2005

[16] Siemens, "Profinet Answers for Industry," https://w3.siemens.com/mcms/water-industry/en/Documents/PROFINET.pdf, 2010, Accessed 28.01.2016

[17] EtherCAT Technology Group, "Moving up to Industrial Ethernet," Industrial Ethernet Book, Issue 45/35, 2016

[18] Rockwell Automation, "Fundamentals of Ethernet/IP Network Technology," Rockwell Automation presentation, TechED 2015

[19] Jari Ahokas, "Secure and Reliable Communications Solution for SCADA and PPDR Use," Master's Thesis, Laurea University of Applied Sciences, 2013

[20] C. Hauser, D. Bakken, I. Dionysiou, K. Gjermundrřd, V. Irava, and A. Bose, "Security, Trust and QoS in next-generation control and communication for large power systems," International Journal of Critical Infrastructures, Volume 4, Issue 1-2, 2008

[21] N. Barkakati and G. C. Wilshusen, "Deficient ICT Controls Jeopardize Systems Supporting the Electric Grid: A Case Study," Securing Electricity Supply in the Cyber Age, Springer, 2009, pp. 129-142

[22] J. Bilbao, C. Cruces, and I. Armendariz, "Methodology for the QoS Characterization in High Constraints Industrial Networks," Open Journal of Communications and Software, Volume 1, Number 1, 2014, pp. 30-41

[23] J. Beran, and F. Zezulka, "Evaluation of Real-Time Behavior in Virtual Automation Networks," Proceedings of the 17th World Congress of The International Federation of Automatic Control, Seoul, Korea, 2008

[24] V. Skendzic, I. Ender, and G. Zweigle, "IEC 61850-9-2 Process Bus and Its Impact on Power System Protection and Control Reliability," in proceedings of the 9th Annual Western Power Delivery Automation Conference, April 3-5, 2007, Spokane, USA

[25] M. Rensburg, D. Dolezilek, and J. Dearien, "Case Study: Using IEC 61850 Network Engineering Guideline Test Procedures to Diagnose and Analyze Ethernet Network Installations," in proceedings of PAC World Africa 2015, November 12-13., Johannesburg, South Africa

[26] A. Al-Fuqaha, M. Guizani, M. Mohammadi, M. Aledhari, and M. Ayyash, "Internet of Things: A Survey on Enabling Technologies, Protocols, and Applications," IEEE Communication Surveys and Tutorials, Vol. 17, No. 4, 2015, pp. 2347-2376

[27] Open Networking Foundation, "Software-Defined Networking: The New Norm for Networks white paper," https://www.opennetworking.org/images/stories/downloads/sdn-resources/white-papers/wp-sdn-newnorm.pdf, Accessed 28.01.2016.

[28] Industrial Ethernet Book, "Quality of Service for high priority networks," http://www.iebmedia.com/index.php?id=5594&parentid=63&themeid=255&showdetail=true, accessed: 08.09.2016

[29] P. Blanco, G. A. Lewis, and P. Merson, "Service Level Agreements in Service-Oriented Architecture Environments," Technical Note, Software Engineering Institute, CMU/SEI-2008-TN-021

[30] R.C. Parks and E. Rogers, "Best practices in automation security," Security & Privacy, IEEE (Volume:6 , Issue: 6), 2009, pp 37-43

[31] G. Blank, "Object-oriented Software Engineering," http://www.cse.lehigh.edu/~glennb/oose/figs/pfleeger/Vmodel.jpg, Accessed 18.03.2016.

[32] D. Cronberger, "The software-defined Industrial Network," The Industrial Ethernet Book, Issue 84, 2014, pp. 8-13

iaria journals

www.iariajournals.org

International Journal On Advances in Intelligent Systems
issn: 1942-2679

International Journal On Advances in Internet Technology
issn: 1942-2652

International Journal On Advances in Life Sciences
issn: 1942-2660

International Journal On Advances in Networks and Services
issn: 1942-2644

International Journal On Advances in Security
issn: 1942-2636

International Journal On Advances in Software
issn: 1942-2628

International Journal On Advances in Systems and Measurements
issn: 1942-261x

International Journal On Advances in Telecommunications
issn: 1942-2601